In case of loss, please return to:

_____

_____

_____

_____

As a reward: $ _____

D1398190

JEN HATMAKER

BESTSELLING AUTHOR OF 7

INTER-RUPTED

WHEN JESUS WRECKS YOUR COMFORTABLE CHRISTIANITY

Published by LifeWay Press®
© 2012 Jen Hatmaker
Reprinted 2014

No part of this work may be reproduced or transmitted in any form or
by any means, electronic or mechanical, including photocopying and
recording, or by any information storage or retrieval system, except as
may be expressly permitted in writing by the publisher. Requests for
permission should be addressed in writing to LifeWay Press®, One
LifeWay Plaza, Nashville, TN 37234-0152.

ISBN: 978-1-4300-4225-9
Item: 005744570

Dewey decimal classification number: 234.2
Subject heading: FAITH \ CHRISTIAN LIFE

Printed in the United States of America.

Young Adult Ministry Publishing
LifeWay Church Resources
One LifeWay Plaza
Nashville, Tennessee 37234-0152

We believe the Bible has God for its author; salvation for its end; and truth,
without any mixture of error, for its matter and that all Scripture is totally
true and trustworthy. To review LifeWay's doctrinal guideline, please visit
www.lifeway.com/doctrinalguideline.

Unless otherwise indicated, all Scripture quotations are taken from the Holman
Christian Standard Bible®, copyright © 1999, 2000, 2002, 2003 by Holman Bible
Publishers. Used by permission. Holman Christian Standard Bible®, Holman CSB®,
and HCSB® are federally registered trademarks of Holman Bible Publishers. Other
versions include: NIV, the Holy Bible, New International Version, copyright © 1973,
1978, 1984 by International Bible Society. Scripture taken from the New American
Standard Bible®, copyright © 1960, 1962, 1963, 1968, 1971, 1972, 1973, 1975, 1977,
1995 by the Lockman Foundation. Used by permission. (*www.lockman.org*).

Cover illustration and design by The Visual Republic.

TABLE OF CONTENTS

ICON LEGEND

 Things to
listen to

 Things
to watch

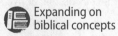 Expanding on
biblical concepts

 On the Web

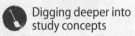 Digging deeper into
study concepts

 Additional
Resources

MEET THE AUTHOR

My name is Jen Hatmaker. I happily live in Austin, Texas, where our city motto is "Keep Austin Weird." (I am certainly doing my part.) My husband, Brandon, and I have five kids. Three the old-fashioned way—Gavin, Sydney, and Caleb—and two through adoption from Ethiopia—Ben and Remy. Most days, Brandon and I wake up, look each other in the eye, and burst out laughing. We gave God a list of things we would and wouldn't do years ago, and He didn't listen to any of it.

Brandon and I joined the adventurous, neurotic world of missional church planters in March 2008 when we started Austin New Church, a community of faith obsessed about bringing justice and restoration to the city and the world. God continues to move mightily through our young church despite the good to excellent chance we have of sabotaging it.

I've written eight other books and Bible studies, including *The Modern Girl's Guide to Bible Study* series and *7: An Experimental Mutiny Against Excess*. I travel all over the United States speaking at conferences and retreats, even to Iowa during a blizzard though I don't own a coat (Austin may be weird, but it's warm). If you "get me" and would like me to speak at your thing, go to *jenhatmaker.com* for more details.

Life Interrupted.

Welcome.

It is with something of an obsession that I've written *Interrupted*. There is no other message, no competing subject, nothing else but this extraordinary story God recently wrote into my family's script. This is the unplugged version of how God interrupted our typical American life and sent us in a direction we couldn't even imagine. If I seem to have tunnel vision, all I can say is that's what happens when God shouts in your face and demands entire life change. I am fixated, and the only objective as central as living out this new mandate is mobilizing others to join me.

Let me say at the outset, right at the beginning of what I hope becomes an interruption in your life, that I love and believe in the church. The church is God's vehicle to change the world. And though I'm critical at times of us, as the church, I am so because I dream about what the church could and should be. But until we are all compelled and contributing members of the body of Jesus, we'll have to settle for an anemic faith and a church that robs Christ-followers of their vitality and repels the rest of the world. There is a call on our generation that must be answered by us collectively. Sequestering into our tribes, staying safely inside the walls of our buildings, is a luxury we no longer have. We are at the tipping point when everyone has to grab an oar.

It is with great anticipation that I enter this discussion with you. You'll find I don't peddle fluff, and when not being sarcastic, I'm dead serious about the gospel and the church in this postmodern world. This book you're holding represents the most transformational message I've ever encountered, and I'd been a believer for 28 years, a pastor's daughter, a pastor's wife, and author of six Christian books before I stumbled on it.

One last note on what this project is not: It is not a how-to manual. It is not an authoritative program for living missionally. It is not an expert's opinion on church trends and postmodernist thought. It is not a raging deconstruction or a soft-sell relativist approach. I am a bumbling, fumbling, searching, questioning sojourner.

I have some churchy credentials, but they are irrelevant to the arc of this story. So if you're looking for a mentor or professional or someone who has already landed, put this book down and buy something by Ed Stetzer or John Piper.

However, if you're navigating the tension between your Bible and your life, or Jesus' ancient ideas and the modern wayward church, or God's kingdom on earth

IF YOU HAVE LOOKED AT THE CHURCH AT LARGE, THE CURRENT PRESENTATION OF "A GOOD, OBEDIENT LIFE," OR THE CHRISTIAN EFFECT ON CULTURE AND ASKED, "IS THIS ALL THERE IS?" THEN YOU'RE IN THE RIGHT PLACE.

and reality, then welcome. Sometimes it's better to wade through murky waters with a fellow explorer than with an authority. Questions can still be investigated with another learner rather than with one who has only answers. There is much value in the struggle. I may not offer resolution, but I will humbly and gratefully enter the conversation with you. If you have looked at the church at large, the current presentation of "a good, obedient life," or the Christian effect on culture and asked, "Is this all there is?" then you're in the right place.

So then, let me tell you how my comfortable, consumer life was interrupted, and perhaps yours will be, too.

BRANDON'S TAKE

I'm Brandon Hatmaker, Jen's husband, and from time to time in your study I'll show up to give you my take on these life interruptions.

Most of us look at change as a threat. And why not? It's foreign and jacks up what we know and like. It makes the consistent inconsistent. It typically removes comfort. But change is not a threat. It's a fact. If we act as if change just happens upon us—surprise!—in a sudden upheaval, we miss its continuing flow, its lessons, and the opportunity to keep up with it. Change is a fact of life. Throughout history, we've seen shifts in our culture, our communities, the way we think, and the way we express our faith; whether it comes from a revolution, a movement, or a ripple. Change is a reality, and we're living right in the middle of it.

The good news is that God can be found right in the middle of it as well. God does not change, but He uses change . . . to change us. He sends us on journeys that bring us to the end of ourselves. We often feel out of control, yet if we embrace His leading, we may find ourselves on the ride of our lives.

There is a change happening in our generation marked by a shift in thinking; a shift central to the missional church. Thus, it is essential to those seeking to live on mission. This became personal for Jen and me in 2007, and it came with some major changes.

Living on mission goes far beyond the "what and how" of being sent, but hinges on the "who" of other people. It's about intentionally living the gospel wherever you are. This comes at great cost, but we've seen this posture become a catalyst for genuine life change.

This book is about the journey of journey. Through it, a local church emerged and kingdom partnerships began. However, while it chronicles the birth of Austin New Church, this story mostly tells how our lives were interrupted and changed forever. On the journey, we became learners again; we learned to be people who are becoming. It tells of new hearts and new minds, permission that comes from a "new command," and the discovery of an ancient way that is constantly made new again.

It was a profound moment when we realized this wasn't just about us or even our church. It was far bigger than that. We've found these changes happening in the hearts of believers around the world. We suspect many of you will relate.

Our hope is that through our story, you might identify where God is leading you. We hope you read something that helps you overcome what is holding you back. And we give you permission to chase after it.

SESSION ONE
POOR

No matter how many Februaries my son Gavin navigates in public school with the month-long focus on black history, he cannot grasp the concept of racism. In first grade, he came home chattering about "Martin," and deep discussion ensued. When I asked why Martin was so mistreated, Gavin was clueless, so I suggested it was his black skin color. Gavin rolled his eyes and responded, "Geez, Mom. He wasn't black. He was brown." Indeed.

In February of second grade, Gavin came home with fresh indignation. "Mom, thank goodness we didn't live in Martin's time, because me and Dad couldn't be together!" *Why not?* I asked. "Duh! Because Dad has *black* hair!" The term *black* obviously applied to any old body part—the civil rights crisis seemed fairly broad in his estimation.

Last year in fourth grade, when surely the world had ruined his innocence on this matter, I was surprised to hear this from Gavin: "Whew! Good thing we live in the new millennium, Mom. If we lived back in the olden days, me and Noah"—his very white, blond, blue-eyed friend up the street—"would've had to go to different schools!" I asked why he thought they'd be separated, and his answer was, "I have no idea, but for some reason no one got to go to school together back then. They just split everybody up! It was a crazy time, Mom."

How do you explain the civil rights movement to a child? If you're interested, pick up a copy of *Martin's Big Words*, a children's book by Doreen Rappaport. In it, she blends narrative with Dr. King's own words to tell the story of his life.

The American Dream has meant many things to many different people, but its origin is with the founding fathers who wrote about the opportunity for "life, liberty, and the pursuit of happiness" in the Declaration of Independence. By the 1960s, the dream was largely thought of in terms of material gain.

BLACK AND WHITE

Gavin doesn't get it because he has no personal exposure to the central issue of racism. Because he doesn't understand the core matter, all these subsequent factoids just float around. Sure, he's upset about them, but he doesn't really grasp their significance because he doesn't understand what's in the middle of it all.

Likewise, I still can't believe it, but I managed to attend church three times a week as a fetus, fulfill the "pastor's kid" role growing up, graduate from a Baptist college, marry a pastor, serve in full-time ministry for 12 years, and become a Christian author and speaker—but I missed the main point. I now read treasured, even memorized Scriptures and realize I never understood what they really meant.

Until a few years ago, my life resembled the basic pursuit of the American Dream, only it occurred in a church setting. Here's what it looked like: Go to college, get married, have kids, make good money, progress up the neighborhood ladder, amass beautiful things, keep our life safe and protected, raise smart children to be wildly successful and never move back home, serve at church more than makes sense, and eventually retire in comfort.

That's how we lived, and that's just how I liked it—safe and prosperous. Outside of our obligatory 10 percent tithe, we spent our money how we wanted (on ourselves), and I could live an "obedient life" without sacrificing the lifestyle I craved.

What does the American Dream mean to you?

Does that idea square with biblical values? Why or why not?

How do you think the American Dream has influenced the goals of individual believers? How about the goals of churches?

In my American Dream, I considered the church campus to be the center of all things spiritual. In other words, if you needed some help, guidance, or understanding, then you came to the church building. Once you did, those of us already there would pour our lives out in an attempt to disciple you and build spiritual health into your life. All this would take place on a church campus and through church programs.

My pastor husband and I worked hard at this philosophy. We spent every waking moment with Christians and all our efforts serving the "Already Convinced." We were so busy serving believers, in fact, that it never occurred to us to imagine a different way of not only doing church, but of doing life.

And yet for me, something was off about the way we were living, beginning with the fact that we were far too consumed with worthless things. We spent an unhealthy amount of time dreaming about our next house, our next financial increase, and our next level of living. We were the opposite of counterculture. We were a mirror image of culture, just a churched-up version.

Something was off about our church life, too. Like why wouldn't people commit to our church programs, despite the endless work poured into them? And why did 70 percent of the initial enthusiasts drop out by the end? Why did the same people end up doing everything? Why did so many leave claiming they needed more when we were all working 80 hours a week to meet their needs? Why couldn't I recall the last person I led to Christ? Why did I spend all my time blessing blessed people who should have been on the giving side of the equation by then?

Why did I feel so dry?

Can you relate to any of those questions? Which ones? Why?

Ⓡ If you want more insight into why young adults are either coming to or avoiding church, pick up a copy of *Lost and Found* by Ed Stetzer. It contains research and insight into the current trends of church attendance among young adults.

Have you ever had a moment when you felt spiritually dry? What happened?

You can learn more about Shane Claiborne's life, message, and ministry by visiting *thesimpleway.org*, where their motto is simple: "Dream big. Live small."

READER BEWARE: LIFE-ALTERING PRAYER AHEAD . . .

Emerging from a two-month sabbatical from writing and traveling, I was stunned to discover that I felt neither rested nor restored. I felt dry as the desert. I later read a perfect summation of my angst by Shane Claiborne in *The Irresistible Revolution*:

"I developed a spiritual form of bulimia where I did my devotions, read all the new Christian books and saw the Christian movies, and then vomited information up to friends, small groups, and pastors. But it never had the chance to digest. I had gorged myself on all the products of the Christian industrial complex but was spiritually starving to death. I was marked by an overconsumption but malnourished spiritually, suffocated by Christianity but thirsty for God."[1]

Though I couldn't articulate it at the time, this was what I felt. I couldn't determine the cause yet, but I felt the hunger in the pit of my stomach.

> **What do you think Claiborne meant by "suffocated by Christianity but thirsty for God"?**

> **Can you identify with that sentiment? Why or why not?**

For a humorous look inside the Christian subculture, check out the daily blog from *stuffchristianslike.net*. Be prepared to get made fun of.

Let me paint the picture of a life-changing morning: I was driving home with my three kids. It was not a holy moment. It was not some silent, sacred encounter with the Spirit. There was no fasting or meditation. As my kids were squawking in the back, I prayed a one-line prayer (and I strongly advise against this prayer unless you are quite ready for God to take you seriously and wreck your plans): "God, raise up in me a holy passion."

What I really meant by that prayer was, "God, give me happy feelings." I was not seriously asking for intervention that would require anything of me. Hardly. "Holy passion" meant "pull me out of this funk with your Magic Happiness Wand." Was that too much to ask? Evidently, God had a different idea, and the deconstruction of my life began in John 21 where He turned my undiagnosed tension into a full-blown spiritual crisis.

HOLY PASSION MEETS REMEDIAL SHEPHERD

John 21 occurred at a pivotal moment in Peter's life. After denying Christ three times, Jesus was re-commissioning Peter to be the guy and leader Jesus wanted him to be. Never one to waste words, Jesus used specific language, and as I read this passage, I was certain the Lord was about to re-commission my family and me, too.

Read John 21:15-17. Why do you think Jesus asked Peter the same question three times?

To get him to think about the question
To connect the

What emotions do you think Jesus triggered in Peter by the repetition?

I felt Jesus' words targeting me as I read the text: "Jen, do you truly love Me more than anything?" My reaction? Shock. *Seriously? Do I really love You? Are you serious, Jesus?* If I was being honest, I felt a little insulted, kind of injured.

To have my love for Jesus called into question was surprising, and not in the good way. I have plenty of questionable attributes, no doubt, but I sincerely adore Jesus. I told Him as much, too. With no small amount of indignation, I touted my affection for Him with all the self-righteous, sanctimonious ire I could muster. It was a compelling presentation, Oscar-worthy, but it did nothing to end this train wreck of a conversation, because the next verse was worse.

"'Yes, Lord,' he said to Him, 'You know that I love You.'" *[Which was exactly what I said but with more melodrama.]* "'Feed My lambs,' He told him."

"When they had eaten breakfast, Jesus asked Simon Peter, 'Simon, son of John, do you love Me more than these?' 'Yes, Lord,' he said to Him, 'You know that I love You'" (John 21:15).

In the encounter between Jesus and Peter, it's interesting to note that the two used different words for love. Jesus asked Peter whether Peter loved (*agape*) Him, and Peter responded that he loved (*phileo*) Jesus. The word *agape* refers to the perfect, Christ-like kind of love. Peter's love, he acknowledged, fell short of that. It was *phileo* love, or love expressed between friends.

What does Jesus' response to Peter indicate to you?

What do you think Jesus meant specifically by "feeding His lambs"?

If you were Peter, what sorts of things would come to mind if you heard "feed My lambs"?

"Jen, feed My lambs." What?

I do feed Your lambs! I feed them spiritually. I herd them into Bible studies and unleash a campaign of harassment when they wander. I counsel and pray and cry and struggle with them. Everyone I know has my number and evidently isn't afraid to use it. I don't know if You noticed, Jesus, but I write Christian books YOU told me to write! I travel and feed sheep all over the nation!

Jesus wasn't finished though—not with Peter, and not with me. Jesus asked a second and third time if Peter really loved Him. And as I processed that repeated question, I sympathized with Peter after time number three:

"Peter [Jen] was grieved that He asked him [her] the third time, 'Do you love Me?'"
"Lord, You know everything! You know that I love You."
"'Feed My sheep,' Jesus said."

The imagery of Jesus as the shepherd and people as His sheep is found consistently through the Gospels. For some other examples, read the parable in Luke 15:3-7 and Jesus' teaching in John 10:1-18.

I think our natural tendency is to treat our spiritual lives as endless efforts in trying harder. But we rarely stop to question whether we're trying hard at the right thing. That's why I was so shocked by what came next. I told Him one last time: "I thought I was feeding Your sheep, but I'll try harder." And this is what I heard in response:

"You do feed souls, but 24,000 of My sheep will die today because no one fed their bellies. Eighteen thousand of them are My youngest lambs, starving today in a world with plenty of food to go around. If you truly love Me, you will *feed My lambs*. My people are crumbling and dying and starving, and you're blessing blessed people and dreaming about your next house."

I couldn't have been more floored if I had come home to find Jesus Himself making homemade salsa in my kitchen. It dawned on me that Jesus was not asking me to do more of the same, but engage a different charge altogether.

It was such a Peter moment, because he was devoted to Jesus, too, but he was misguided. He'd spent three years following his version of the Messiah, only to discover that Jesus had a radically different set of goals than Peter thought. He assumed Jesus was destined for political greatness; that He would somehow bring about the restoration of the nation of Israel. But Jesus had a terribly different set of priorities in mind.

That sounds familiar.

The truth is that in virtually every book in the Bible, God is screaming, begging, pleading, urging us to love mercy and justice, to feed the poor and the orphaned, to care for the last and least. It will not be enough to stand before Jesus one day and say, "Oh, were You serious about all that?"

Is it easier for you to think about feeding the sheep of Jesus in a spiritual sense or a physical sense? Why?

Do you think most of us take issues of mercy and justice seriously enough? Why or why not?

According to *bread.org*, a Web site tracking the worldwide issue of hunger, there are 925 million people in the world who are hungry.

"He has told you men what is good and what it is the LORD requires of you: Only to act justly, to love faithfulness, and to walk humbly with your God" (Micah 6:8).

JAMES, AMOS, JESUS, AND THEM

In humble confession, I've since discovered more than 2,000 Bible verses involving poverty, physical oppression and justice, and the redistribution of resources. Where had I been for 28 years? What Bible was I reading? How had I interpreted those passages as God's intention to bless me a little more than I had already been blessed?

Do you tend to take God's commands regarding justice seriously? Why or why not?

How have you interpreted God's feelings and commands about poverty and suffering? How would you describe His heart on this matter?

The Southern Baptist World Hunger Fund is the only organization in the world that uses 100 percent of all contributions to feed hungry people. Find out more at *worldhungerfund.com*.

Jesus' brother even got in on the action:

"Listen, my dear brothers: Didn't God choose the poor in this world to be rich in faith and heirs of the kingdom that He has promised to those who love Him? Yet you dishonored that poor man . . . If you really carry out the royal law prescribed in Scripture, 'Love your neighbor as yourself,' you are doing well . . . What good is it, my brothers, if someone says he has faith, but does not have works? Can his faith save him? If a brother or sister is without clothes and lacks daily food, and one of you says to them, 'Go in peace, keep warm, and eat well,' but you don't give them what the body needs, what good is it?" (James 2:5-6,8,14-16).

Hey, here's a crazy thought: In the Word, poverty, widows, hunger—these are not metaphors. There are billions of lambs that literally need to be fed. *With food.*

For all my self-proclaimed love of God's Word, what I really loved were the parts that worked for me. For my good. For my blessings. I made it all fit to support my American Dream while keeping my worldview intact.

When have you treated Scripture like a buffet, picking and choosing the parts you like and ignoring the others?

Do you tend to treat statements in the Bible regarding issues like these as literal or metaphorical? Why?

The night before he was assassinated, Dr. Martin Luther King Jr., proclaimed:

"Who is it that is supposed to articulate the longings and aspirations of the people more than the preacher? Somehow the preacher must have a kind of fire shut up in his bones, and whenever injustice is around he must tell it. Somehow the preacher must be an Amos, who said, 'When God speaks, who can but prophesy?' Again with Amos, 'Let justice roll down like waters and righteousness like a mighty stream.' Somehow the preacher must say with Jesus, 'The Spirit of the Lord is upon me, because He hath anointed me, and He's anointed me to deal with the problems of the poor.'"[2] So ... what are the problems of the poor?

WARNING: THE PROBLEMS ARE BAD

Jeffrey Sachs explains in *The End of Poverty*, "If economic development is a ladder with higher rungs representing steps up the path to economic well-being, there are roughly one billion people around the world, one sixth of humanity, who [are] too ill, hungry, or destitute to even get a foot on the first rung of the developmental ladder. These people are the 'poorest of the poor,' or the 'extreme poor' of the planet."[3]

This bottom layer of destitution will never be alleviated without intervention. The majority of the extreme poor are caught in a poverty trap, unable to escape from deprivation because of disease, physical isolation, climate stress, environmental degradation, and poverty itself. Life-saving solutions exist, and most are inexpensive and available, but these families and their governments lack the financial means to obtain them.

Martin Luther King Jr. was a Baptist minister who became a civil rights activist early in his career. He led the 1955 Montgomery Bus Boycott and helped found the Southern Christian Leadership Conference in 1957, serving as its first president. King's efforts led to the 1963 March on Washington, where he delivered his "I Have a Dream" speech. In 1964, King became the youngest person to receive the Nobel Peace Prize for his work to end racial segregation and racial discrimination through civil disobedience and other non-violent means. By the time of his death in 1968, he had refocused his efforts on ending poverty and opposing the Vietnam War, both from a religious perspective.

Jeffrey Sachs is widely considered to be the leading international economic advisor of his generation. Sachs was one of the youngest professors in history at Harvard and is currently the director of the Earth Institute at Columbia University. Find out more about his initiatives at *earth.columbia.edu*.

In Jesus' day, poverty was seen as the disfavor of God. But Jesus radically changed that definition in the Sermon on the Mount, saying that the poor are actually the blessed (Matthew 5:3-12).

The issue of children in crisis is being confronted in many different ways. For example, check out an organization called Sweet Sleep (*sweetsleep.org*), which is committed to tangibly spreading God's love by providing beds for orphaned and abandoned children across the world.

Sachs continues, "A few rungs up the developmental ladder is the upper end of the low-income world, where roughly another 1.5 billion people . . . are 'the poor.' They live above mere subsistence. Although daily survival is pretty much assured, they struggle in the cities and countrysides to make ends meet. Death is not at their door, but chronic financial hardship and a lack of basic amenities such as safe drinking water and functioning latrines are part of their daily lives." Together, the extreme poor (around one billion) and the poor (another 1.5 billion) make up roughly 40 percent of humanity.[4]

Because these numbers are hard to wrap our minds around, let's make this crisis more tangible. If you've lived abroad or have global exposure, the following will be familiar. But if you've never thought critically about the way most of us live, let's for just a second look beyond our lifestyles to see how the rest of the world lives:

* Of the six billion people on planet Earth, about 1.2 billion live on 23 cents a day.
* Half the world lives on less than $2.50 a day.
* The wealthiest one billion people average $70 a day. (This places you and me in the upper, upper, upper percentages of the global population.)
  * If you make $35,000 annually, you are in the top four percent.
  * If you make $50,000 annually, top one percent.
* Someone dies of hunger every 16 seconds.
* Twenty-two million people died of preventable diseases last year; 10 million were children.[5]
* Twenty-seven million children and adults are trapped in slavery because of economic crisis (sex slaves, labor slaves, child soldiers, and child slaves). More slaves exist today than *ever before in human history.*[6]
* More than 143 million children in the world have been orphaned or abandoned (equivalent to more than half the population of the U.S.).
* In the last hour:
  * More than 1,600 children were forced to the streets by the death or abuse of an adult.
  * At least 115 children became prostitutes.
  * More than 66 children younger than 15 years of age were infected with HIV.[7]
* Roughly one billion people in the world do not have suitable housing, and 100 million are entirely homeless.

Clearly, these are the problems of the poor. When God shook Israel awake from her violent slumber, He said:

"Now this was the iniquity of your sister Sodom: She and her daughters had pride, plenty of food, and comfortable security, but didn't support the poor and needy" (Ezekiel 16:49).

I humbly propose that God is calling rich believers in America (which is all of us) to the same reform. I optimistically believe most of us are unconcerned because we're unaware. Toward the goal of global perspective, let's see how the U.S. compares to the rest of the world:

* Forty percent of the world lacks basic water sanitation, resulting in disease, death, wastewater for drinking, and loss of immunity; Americans spent $16 billion on bottled water in 2008.
* We spend more annually on trash bags than nearly half the world spends on all goods combined.
* Four out of five children worldwide work every day instead of going to school; four out of five Americans are high school graduates.
* Eight percent of the rest of the world owns a car; one-third of all American families own three cars.
* Roughly 40 million people (about seven Jewish Holocausts) die annually from starvation, disease, and malnutrition; 65 percent of U.S. adults and 15 percent of children and adolescents are overweight or obese.
* The U.S. makes up five percent of the global population, but we consume 25 percent of the world's oil, 20 million barrels of oil a day; next is China at just 6.9 million a day.
* When a group of leaders from developing nations begged U.S. government leaders to explore intervention options for their countries in crisis, a U.S. official was quoted as saying: "The American lifestyle is not up for negotiation."[8]

How do these statistics hit you? Is your first instinct defensive? Is it criticism? Is it a desire to take action?

R

Just Courage by Gary Haugen, president of the International Justice Mission, is an easy-to-understand, motivational book. It's a great next step if you're finding your heart being tugged into God's mission of justice.

Can you articulate why you answered like you did?

The television show that has been translated into more languages and syndicated more around the globe than any other in the history of entertainment is "Baywatch." If this is what America is exporting, it's no wonder why the world feels as it does about this country.

It's statistics like this that help us understand why when Americans say "democracy," the world hears "greed." What seems like basic freedom to us sounds like vast consumption to everyone else. Their perception doesn't involve the millions of good, hard-working Americans who give and care; it is largely based on the two disturbing ambassadors that represent our country globally: war and Hollywood. ("Brand America" is clearly in trouble.)

"NAME IT AND CLAIM IT"

But this is more than a public relations crisis for Team USA. As much as we know differently, the world believes we are a Christian nation. Given that belief, it's easy to see how the nations of the world simply cannot square how much money we have with how we spend it. Global church leaders are dumbfounded at our excess while their people are dying and starving, especially when so many leading spiritual voices here are proclaiming the prosperity gospel*:

"I preach that anybody can improve their lives. I think God wants us to be prosperous. I think he wants us to be happy. To me, you need to have money to pay your bills. I think God wants us to send our kids to college." –Joel Osteen, pastor of the biggest mega-church in America[9]

The prosperity gospel* is a stream of theological thought believing that it is God's will for every believer to prosper financially, in health, and in education. Proponents of this way of thinking believe the only thing keeping people from achieving that kind of prosperity is a lack of faith.

"Who would want to get in on something where you're miserable, poor, broke and ugly and you just have to muddle through until you get to heaven? I believe God wants to give us nice things." –Joyce Meyer[10]

"Now, last night we began to deal with the relationship between peace and prosperity . . . and we'll look at it again tonight. It says, 'My soul is far from prosperity.' Why? My soul is far from peace because I forgot prosperity. We established last night that you are not whole until you get your money." –Creflo Dollar, World Changers Church International[11]

How do these leaders explain the economic situation of believers in the developing world? If their theology is right, then God primarily loves and cares about us—not the developing world. And evidently

God wants American kids to go to college, but He's OK with 65 million orphans panhandling in Asia. God wants to give us "nice things" but doesn't feel like helping Africans with things like food and water. It's ridiculous. Or in the words of Rick Warren, pastor of the fourth largest mega-church in America, "This idea that God wants everybody to be wealthy? There is a word for that: baloney. It's creating a false idol. You don't measure your self-worth by your net worth. I can show you millions of faithful followers of Christ who live in poverty. Why isn't everyone in the church a millionaire?"[12]

What does your prayer life reveal about your own desire for prosperity?

Rick Warren, pastor of Saddleback Church, has launched the P.E.A.C.E. Plan, a massive effort to mobilize Christians around the world to address what Warren calls the "five global giants" of spiritual emptiness, corrupt leadership, poverty, disease, and illiteracy by promoting reconciliation, equipping servant leaders, assisting the poor, caring for the sick, and educating the next generation. Find out more at *thepeaceplan.com*.

The world knows about our Jesus. They know about His poverty and love of the underdog. They know He told His followers to care for the poor and to share. They've heard about His radical economic theories and revolutionary redistribution concepts. They might not understand the nuances of His divinity or the various shades of His theology, but they know He was a friend of the oppressed.

So to watch Americans living in excess beyond imagination while the world cries out for intervention is an unbearable tension and utterly misrepresents God's kingdom. While the richest people in the world pray to get richer, the rest of the world endures unimaginable suffering with their faces pressed to the window of our prosperity, and we carry on obliviously. Like Gandhi once famously said, "I like your Christ. I do not like your Christians. Your Christians are so unlike your Christ."[13]

You can read more about attitudes similar to Gandhi's in Dan Kimball's thought-provoking book, *They Like Jesus but Not the Church*.

And frankly, our silence threatens not only the world's poor, but our own security. Colin Powell observed, "We cannot win the war on terrorism until we confront the social and political roots of poverty."[14] When people are impoverished and desperate while knowing we have everything they need in the cushions of our couches, it's easy to see how a tyrannical leader can influence them toward our harm: "I'll feed you and get you a gun. We'll fight greedy America." We'll never be safe while we're ignoring the extreme poverty of everyone else. They kill by violence, but we've let them suffer and die by neglect.

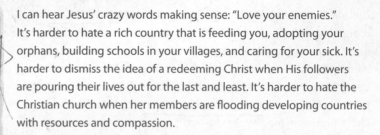

I can hear Jesus' crazy words making sense: "Love your enemies." It's harder to hate a rich country that is feeding you, adopting your orphans, building schools in your villages, and caring for your sick. It's harder to dismiss the idea of a redeeming Christ when His followers are pouring their lives out for the last and least. It's harder to hate the Christian church when her members are flooding developing countries with resources and compassion.

Do you believe there is a link between poverty relief and national security? Why?

"By justice a king brings stability to a land" (Proverbs 29:4).

How might the average citizen of a developing nation respond to our message of prosperity, knowing what they know about the U.S.?

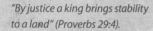

At your small group meeting this week, watch the first session of the documentary feature called "Interrupted—Part I." The video segments are available for purchase on the *Interrupted* product page of *LifeWay.com.*

How might that message affect his or her notion of God?

GIVING THE GOOD STATS SOME PLAY

There is always another side of the story. American philanthropy is legendary, and private giving makes up the brunt of it. The Giving USA Foundation reported that charitable giving in 2006 reached nearly $300 billion; $229 billion given by individuals (as opposed to corporate giving).[15] Much of that charity was domestic, but certainly billions of American dollars reach around the globe annually.

when comparing to others "What's our value on this?"

I also appreciate that thousands of churches are faithfully focused on mission work and foreign relief efforts. Of the $295 billion given to charity in 2006, almost 33 percent of that went to churches, and many use a large portion of those tithes not just for costly overhead and salaries, but for mission work and poverty relief.

I've witnessed people giving so generously of their time, their love, their money, that I've been rendered speechless. Please don't hear me say that America stinks and all her citizens are narcissists. It's just that most of us have no concept of our own prosperity. Nor do we have an accurate understanding of the plight of the rest of the world. Our perspective is limited and our church culture is so consumer-oriented, we're blinded to our responsibility to see God's kingdom come to "all nations," as He was so fond of saying in His Word.

What stand does your church take against poverty and injustice?

Does your church spend most of its time and money on "you" or "them"?

Does that commitment mirror your own commitment to those issues?

A couple recently left our church plant, citing our vision to be missional and socially active: "We believe what you're doing is right, but we're just not motivated by it. I need my pastor to deal with *me*." I had another good friend send an e-mail saying, "You're being so unfair. America gives and gives and gives, and you're making us feel guilty for what we have." I gently asked her to set aside what America is or is not giving and answer for herself: What was *she* doing? Silence.

Listen to "Not Mine Anyway" by JJ Heller from the *Interrupted* playlist. Your group leader can e-mail you the whole playlist, or you can download it for free on the *Interrupted* product page of *LifeWay.com*, under "Support Materials."

John Piper describes the biblical command to go to "all nations" fully and challengingly in his book, *Let the Nations Be Glad*.

And that's really where we are. We stand at the intersection of extreme privilege and extreme poverty, and we have some questions to answer: Do I care? Am I moved by the suffering of all nations? Am I even concerned about the homeless guy on the corner? Am I willing to take the Bible at face value and concur that God is incredibly concerned with social justice? I won't answer one day for the omissions of other people, nor will I get the credit for the general philanthropy of someone else.

It will come down to what *I* did. What *you* did. What we did together.

Of course, all I can do is make the tiniest ripple in the ocean. That's about all you're good for, too. But it's foolish to become paralyzed by the scope of suffering or discouraged by the limit of our reach. Though it's impossible to quantify, it's estimated that roughly 2.1 billion people—about one-third of the planet—identify themselves as Christians.[16] Let's just halve that number to be safe. Imagine if one billion believers obediently decided to become the hands of Christ to this broken world, and most of them had every resource to do it. Then, indeed, we would become "good news to the poor."

Alone, we can affect a few.

But together, we can change the world.

America aside, where do you stand? What does your personal intersection of privilege and poverty look like?

Would you be willing to pray for God to raise up a holy passion in you? If not, what hinders you?

"It is from the numberless diverse acts of courage and belief that human history is shaped. Each time a man stands up for an ideal, or acts to improve the lot of others, or strikes out against injustice, he sends a tiny ripple of hope, and crossing each other from a million different centers of energy and daring, those ripples build a current which can sweep down the mightiest walls of oppression and resistance." –Robert F. Kennedy[17]

BRANDON'S TAKE

In case anyone was wondering, I was completely oblivious to Jen's inner tension during this season. Several years ago, I began noticing a pattern in men, and especially pastors. We tend to make major life decisions and drag our wives along—criticizing their lack of faith or praising their submission—and expect them to just toe the company line. The result? When things go well, great, we're the heroes. But when things go south, we aren't emotionally in it together, and it becomes us against them. Many pastors' wives feel like the church is the other woman. I recently read that 88 percent of pastors' wives answered yes to experiencing periods of depression.

So, I began to pray, "God, don't move in me unless you move in Jen. In fact, for the big things, move in her heart first." I begged Him, "God, don't call me if You don't call my wife, too. If You don't, I'm not going. I'm just gonna read that as if I'm missing it."

God uses women as the catalyst in much of His work. Look in the Scriptures. Look in our churches. It's the women who seem most sensitive to God's Spirit. So if you trust the faith of your wife, why not simply ask God to speak in unison to you both?

Easier said than done? Sometimes. Jen started reading books with hippies on the cover and asking me stuff like, "What if we're missing out on this whole thing?" All along I'm thinking, "Are you kidding me? We're all in! I oversee the spiritual development of a great church that baptized more than 400 people last year! And now you're wondering if we need to change every motivation and method that got us here?"

At this point, it never crossed my mind that a move was on our horizon. But I did know that this was serious for Jen. So I ignored her. And promised I'd read those books and listen to those sermons . . . someday.

NOTES

INTERRUPTING YOUR LIFE

Here are some of the major influences in this part of Jen's story. To go further with some of the ideas from this session, pick one out to dig into yourself:

* *Radical* by David Platt
* *The End of Poverty* by Jeffrey D. Sachs
* *sub-merge* by John B. Hayes
* *A Long Way Gone* by Ishmael Beah
* The Miracle Foundation (*miraclefoundation.org*)

SESSION TWO
LOW

I have a tendency to select friends who are firecrackers. Because my giant personality can cannibalize an introvert, most of my friends are loud and insensitive, just like me. Case in point: My friend Christi recently described a battle between her and her usually mild-mannered hubby, Brett. Typically, he is the ying to her yang; the cool, bubbling stream to her wild, Class 5 rapids. *Usually*.

But recently, Brett was gone on business for a week leaving Christi alone with their two young children. In a burst of good discernment, he let Christi sleep in his first morning back. She walked downstairs to find the kids playing, while Brett read the paper in the kitchen. Recalling that she'd used half a banana the night before, she noticed a new halved banana, while the original, leftover half sat unused on the counter.

Bananas, frustration, and personalities collided in their kitchen. . . .

THE TROUBLE WITH BANANAS

Here's how the interaction went regarding the leftover bananas in question:

Christi: Did you cut that new banana in half?

Brett: Yes.

Christi: What did you do with it?

Brett: I fed the baby, of course!

Christi: Why didn't you use the banana that was already cut? How could you possibly miss the banana half sitting three millimeters away from the whole one?!

Brett: I cut the first banana that I saw!

Christi: We can't just be cutting new bananas all the time when there are perfectly good halves going to waste! We're not millionaires! Think, Brett, think!

[Insert the sound of Brett's psyche snapping like a twig.]

Brett: (Tossing some change from his pocket on the counter.) Here's $0.89. Go buy yourself a whole new bunch of bananas! Sure hope we can still pay the mortgage! Hey kids, guess what? If you drop a piece of banana on the carpet, you're eating it, dog hair and all! We don't waste an ounce of banana in this house! We *steward* our bananas! To whom much has been given, much will be required, and we've been given a ton of bananas, and *we will be found faithful with our bananas!* (Shoving the aforementioned half a banana into his mouth in one bite.) I am eternally grateful for the nourishment of this banana! Daily potassium? *Check!* And, surprisingly, *a full day's worth of vitamin C!* Waste not, want not, *not in this house!*

It was, in short, the banana that broke the camel's back.

Human nature is so hopeless. When we are already idling high, it doesn't take but the slightest provocation for the banana to really hit the fan. Burdened with fatigue or frustrated, things often get worse before they get better. Sometimes we don't gain clarity about our true condition until we suffer a personal Armageddon over produce.

This is precisely how the trajectory of my story went, too. Troubled with fresh conviction and shocking ignorance, the racket in my head grew much louder before it got better. Slamming on the brakes was one thing, but the subsequent direction change was unbelievably chaotic. I found myself crying, hollering, wondering, reading, and struggling about almost every element in my life.

Enjoyed Jen's engaging writing style? Be sure and take a look at the other books and Bible studies she's authored at *jenhatmaker.com*.

So began a period of reorienting my mind in the redemptive mission of Christ. I was convinced of the *need* to change my mind, but what came next was *actually* changing my mind, and I didn't envy God that task.

TEACHING AN OLD DOG NEW TRICKS

I started reading the Bible through a fresh lens, and a theme began to lift from its pages. I began noticing the liberal use of the word "new," particularly once Jesus came on the scene. Since that concept was hitting close to home, I dug in:

* *New* wine has to be poured into *new* wineskins.
* The kingdom of heaven is a storehouse of not just old treasures, but *new* ones too.
* Jesus rolled out a whole *new* teaching.
* We have a *new* and different life linked to the way Jesus lived and died.
* We're supposed to be serving in a *new* way, the way of the Spirit.
* All our rules mean nothing; the only thing that matters is being a *new* kind of human.
* Part of our salvation is having a *new* attitude about things.

Read Luke 5:27-39. What do Jesus' relationships reveal to you about His character?

> He wasn't afraid of anyones bad habits rubbing off on him. He new who he was + could love people the way they were.

Considering the crowd and context, what do you think Jesus was trying to communicate with the "new wine in new wineskins" illustration?

> you can't expect new christians to behave as old Christians. The must grow in a process to get there.

How do you think that illustration relates to you personally? What "new wine" might God be wanting to pour into your life?

In his commentary on the Book of Luke, Max Anders states: "New wine expands as it settles into the bottle. It needs new wineskins that have the resiliency to stretch and expand with the new wine. Old skins will not work. They are too set in their ways. They will cause you to lose all the wine. Old power structures built on human wisdom and human control will not work. So choose the power you want to follow: the lifestyle of the set-in-their-ways Pharisees and religious leaders with its wine, bread, and comfort—or do you prefer God's call to be persecuted, even killed on a cross for Jesus' sake?"[19]

Jesus' teaching regarding new wine is recorded in three out of the four Gospels—Matthew 9; Mark 2; and Luke 5.

As a vessel, are you more like an old wineskin, having trouble expanding with the new wine? Or are you more like a new wineskin, able to stretch and grow with new ideas and convictions? Why?

Conversion "refers to a decisive turning from sin to faith in Jesus Christ as the only means of salvation. It is a once-for-all unrepeatable and decisive act. One is either converted or not."[21]

Even though I'd read passages like these dozens—maybe even hundreds—of times, the concept of "new" began to trouble me for the first time. Let's go old school and peek at the actual definition: "other than the former or the old; different and better."[20] This is a continuous process with Jesus—He's always bursting out of the old into the new. For me, "old" meant a life ungoverned by Jesus' principles. The kind of life Jesus introduced was new; everything outside of that was old.

Perhaps the synonym for "new" that most grieved me was "different." Although parts of my life were different than your average Westerner, most really weren't. I went to church way more than a normal human would or should, but I still had too much self-absorption, debt, and pride just like everyone else. I lived for me and mine. Outside of my spiritual titles—pastor's wife, Bible teacher, Christian author and speaker—there were no radical lifestyle distinctions that would cause anyone to say, "Wow. You live a really different life."

How would an impartial observer assess your life?

"Therefore if anyone is in Christ, there is a new creation; old things have passed away, and look, new things have come" (2 Corinthians 5:17).

If someone had to sum you up only by watching your actions, what would they conclude?

I realized I was completely normal. But my Savior was the most "un-normal" guy ever. And it was *His* un-normal ideas that made everything new.

Jesus never fit in. He was never the cool guy. He was always wrecking everyone's way of thinking. I'm positive the disciples sat on pins and needles when Jesus talked to a crowd, worried what crazy thing He might say next. (Nice: "I am the Bread of life." Minutes later: "Unless you eat the flesh of the Son of Man and drink His blood, you have no life in you." Mass exodus ensues.)

But it wasn't just what He said; it was what He did. It was who He spent time with, talked to, and argued with, to say nothing of His very un-affluent life. If we took Jesus' teachings away and just focused on the way He lived, He would still be radical.

If we didn't have record of Jesus' words but only His actions, what kind of conclusions would you draw?

What and who would you conclude was most important to Him? Why?

DESIRING, DOING, AND REMEMBERING

I re-discovered another passage in Luke 22, the story of Jesus' final meal with His disciples, a meal Jesus used to help close the normal/un-normal gap. This is the seventh recorded meal scene in Luke and two more remain. Evidently, Luke loved meals. So much happened around the dinner table.

What are we supposed to learn from Luke's emphasis on meals?

Where does the majority of ministry happen now? What have we replaced the dinner table with? Why?

Much of the controversy in Luke 5 involved Jesus' relationships. He was associating with tax collectors who were notorious liars and cheaters, intensely disliked and distrusted by everyone. If that weren't bad enough, Jesus was actually having table fellowship with "sinners" like these tax collectors. To eat with someone in that culture indicated a large step beyond mere acquaintance; it indicated intimacy.

Throughout the Bible, God commemorated significant events using food. To learn more about the major feasts of the Jewish calendar and their significance to Christianity, check out *Feast*, a Bible study by Derek Leman, at *threadsmedia.com*.

Read Luke 22:13-16. What are your initial impressions?

Passover is the yearly celebration of God's deliverance of the Israelites from slavery in Egypt. The meal helps us remember the night when the Israelites put lamb's blood on their doorposts, causing the angel of death to pass over their houses. That night, every firstborn in Egypt was struck dead, save those protected by the blood. Read the account in Exodus 11–12.

Jesus was seriously making a point with His statement in verse 15. In Greek, He literally said, "I have desired with desire to eat this Passover with you." Jesus was underscoring His great anticipation for this moment. He had been waiting, and this was it. This was monumental. He would become living theology to change the course of history. It was time to make old things brand spanking new.

Read Luke 22:17-19 and John 6:48-60. Why do you think this was considered such a hard teaching for not only Jesus' skeptics but also His disciples?

Why is it still hard for us?

This was a radical moment for the disciples. Jesus redefined a Jewish ritual with a 1500-year history. In a culture that revered ancient feasts and festivals *as is*, Jesus transformed the untransformable. It's hard to imagine how bizarre this must have sounded to the disciples, which helps us understand why they shifted their focus to arguing about "Top Disciple" three minutes later.

"This is My body. This is My blood."

Jesus didn't just host and serve the meal; He became the meal. He was the sacrificial Lamb, broken for the redemption of humanity, forever our feast and sustenance. He was the sacrifice, the High Priest and Reigning King. He alone understood the necessary tension between His submission and dominion. The Lamb went willingly, embracing sacrifice.

"No one takes [My life] from Me, but I lay it down on My own" (John 10:18).

That's right, Judas. You were but a pawn in the sovereign plan of the Most High. The singular reason you were allowed near Jesus in betrayal was because this was your preordained hour of darkness—not before or after. The angry mob didn't "catch" Jesus. The high priest didn't decide His fate. The false witnesses, Herod, Pilate, soldiers—none took His life. Jesus eluded death countless times before the cross.

He laid His own life down at the appointed time—not under coercion or because His reckless message finally caught up with Him. Jesus assured us that every time it seemed He was forced against His will, He wasn't. He chose and embraced that moment. It was the culmination of God's redemptive plan for mankind. All of heaven waited with baited breath as the King became the Lamb and humanity was finally rescued.

Jesus desired with desire to offer His body, His blood—this bread, this cup.

Why is it significant that Jesus willingly gave up His life?

Why do you think He chose to commemorate that event with food?

"Do this in remembrance of Me" (Luke 22:19). Here I got stuck. Do what? What did He mean by *do*? Is this a simple matter of observing the Lord's Supper once a quarter? Was Jesus emphasizing the Jewish custom of ritual, just with new symbolism?

The important "do" aspect is how Jesus used the present tense, indicating continuous action, as opposed to the aorist imperative, implying a single action. *(What?)* It's the difference between "I'm going to Sonic" and "I'm going crazy." Once versus perpetual. When Jesus said of the wine in verse 17, "Take this and share it among yourselves," that

"The Son of Man will go away as it has been determined" (Luke 22:22).

Jesus' words that night have been a source of church division for centuries. The issue in question is whether the words, "This is My body" are literal. Some believe that when believers partake in communion, the elements actually become the body and blood of Christ. This is called transubstantiation. Others hold that Jesus' words were symbolic, much in the same way that He called Himself the Good Shepherd or the Bread of life.

was a one-time command. But when He said, "Do this in remembrance of Me," it required continuous action.

What does Jesus' command mean to you?

"On the night when He was betrayed, the Lord Jesus took bread, gave thanks, broke it, and said, 'This is My body, which is for you. Do this in remembrance of Me'" (1 Corinthians 11:23-24).

How have you interpreted that command in the past?

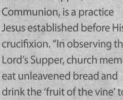

The Lord's Supper, or Communion, is a practice Jesus established before His crucifixion. "In observing the Lord's Supper, church members eat unleavened bread and drink the 'fruit of the vine' to symbolize the body and blood of Christ. This memorial meal is to be observed until Christ comes again. The frequency among churches for observing the Lord's Supper varies, but the Scripture does require that it be done regularly."[23]

Not only does Jesus' statement require a constant response, but "remembrance" is from the Greek *anamnesis* meaning "to make real." Communion is more than a memory, more than a reverent moment when we recall Jesus' heroic sacrifice. Remembrance means honoring Jesus' mercy mission with tangible, physical action since it was a tangible, physical sacrifice. In other words, "Constantly make this real."

That's the command of Jesus.

Not only was Communion a symbolic ritual, but it was a new prototype of discipleship. "Continuously make my sacrifice real, by doing *this very thing*." But what? What was the very thing Jesus was doing? He was becoming broken and poured out for hopeless people. He was becoming a living offering, denying Himself for the salvation and restoration of humanity. Obedience to Jesus' command is more than looking backward; it's a present and continuous replication of His sacrifice. We don't simply remember the meal; we become the meal too.

"Now you are the body of Christ" (1 Corinthians 12:27).

Doesn't this concept of being broken for others ring true? It's a spiritual dynamic manifested physically. Why is it so exhausting to uphold someone's heavy, inconvenient burden? Why are you spent from shouldering someone's grief or being an armor-bearer? Why is it that lifting someone out of his or her rubble leaves you breathless? Because you are part of the body of Christ, broken and poured out, just like He was. Mercy has a cost: Someone must be broken for someone else to be fed. The sermon that changed your life? That messenger was poured out so you could hear it. The friends who stood in the gap during your crisis? Each embraced some sacrifice of brokenness for your healing. Anytime you say, "That fed me; that nourished me," someone was the broken bread for your fulfillment.

When were you fed by someone else's brokenness?

Recently, when have you poured yourself out for another to be fed?

"Carry each other's burdens, and in this way you will fulfill the law of Christ" (Galatians 6:2).

Carrying on the life of Christ is integrated with the concept of death. There is a death/life rhythm that sustains creation. Much like a seed is destroyed to produce a living tree, or a vegetable is plucked from its vine to nourish a living body, self-sacrifice is hardwired into the mission of a believer. It's paradoxical, but it fits into the economy of God. Think about it—it's only through death that we see life. It's only through weakness that we see strength. It's only through meekness that we see power.

That helps me better understand Paul's teaching to the Corinthian church:

"We always carry the death of Jesus in our body, so that the life of Jesus may also be revealed in our body. For we who live are always given over to death because of Jesus, so that Jesus' life may also be revealed in our mortal flesh. So death works in us, but life in you" (2 Corinthians 4:10-12).

Death in me = life in you.
Broken so someone else is fed.
"Feed My lambs."

TOUGH CROWD

I was connecting the dots and realized I had a situation on my hands. If I was to "do this in remembrance of Jesus," with the same motive and manner, I had to address some hard questions.

Starting with: Who was Jesus broken and poured out for? Luke tells us Jesus said "for you." Matthew and Mark report Him saying "for many." Certainly the disciples sitting there were part of that group. That entourage had their flaws (clearly), but you have to acknowledge that they loved and followed Jesus. They embraced some element of self-denial to be His protégés. These are people I like to think of Jesus dying for. You know, the ones who wrote a bunch of the Bible later; the ones who died for their faith and such.

If I'm honest, these are also the types I wanted to be broken for. If I'm picking who I sacrifice for, I'm thinking: future martyrs, gospel writers, and/or world changers. I love to pour into believers who take Jesus seriously—eager learners who pester me with burning questions about Scripture that keep them up at night. These are my kinds of people. It's easier to serve the convinced who prefer a table in the Upper Room.

As a living offering, are you the broken bread mainly for other believers and church programs?

"Make your own attitude that of Christ Jesus, who, existing in the form of God, did not consider equality with God as something to be used for His own advantage. Instead He emptied Himself by assuming the form of a slave, taking on the likeness of men. And when He had come as a man in His external form, He humbled Himself by becoming obedient to the point of death—even death on a cross" (Philippians 2:5-8).

What are the benefits to serving the "Already Convinced"?

Here's the problem: Judas was also part of the "for you" group Jesus referred to. If the other disciples represented people eager to follow and learn and love, Judas represented those who would turn on me in spite of what I sacrificed or why.

If I didn't grasp that then, I'm getting it now, thanks to people like the homeless man I served a burger to in 105° heat who told me, "I hope this satisfies your white guilt for the day." And the addict we supported in every conceivable way who went back to heroin and never called again. And the young man we helped out of the shelter who spent the money we gave him on new piercings and a Bluetooth. And the believers who thought we were crazy.

This was one reason I was detached from the margins—irresponsibility, recklessness, and thanklessness: *They'll spend it on booze. Government is corrupt and shouldn't be helped. Get off your lazy butt and get a job and then we'll talk.* I was shockingly ignorant about the cycles of poverty and addiction. (During the 2008 presidential election, a girl I know posted online: "Hey, poor people! Here's some advice: Have the good common sense not to get sucked into poverty!" I almost shoved my head through a plate glass window.)

What did God teach me through Judas-at-Jesus'-table, eating the broken bread that was His body? We don't get to opt out of living on mission because we may not be appreciated. We're not allowed to neglect the oppressed because we have reservations about their discernment. We can't deny love because it may be despised or misunderstood. We can't withhold social relief because we're not convinced it will be perfectly managed. Must we be wise? Absolutely. But doing nothing is a blatant sin of omission.

Jesus came to the foulest, filthiest place possible, full of ungrateful, self-destructive people who betray Him far more than they love Him: Earth, a whole planet of Judases. He broke His body for rich people who curse Him the second their prosperity is endangered. He poured His blood out for those who take His Word and use it as a bludgeoning tool. He became the offering for people who slander His name with ferocity, while His grace is theirs for the asking until they draw their last breath, even if all they can offer Him in the end is a lifetime of hatred and one moment of repentance.

When Jesus' followers asked what to do about the weeds in the harvest field, He said treat them the same as the wheat, because "when you gather up the weeds, you might also uproot the wheat with them" (Matthew 13:29). I assure you, for every weed who will take advantage of your mercy, there are 50 stalks of wheat who'll shed tears of gratitude for it. There was one Judas, but 11 disciples who were forever transformed by Jesus' broken body. The risk of encountering a few weeds is not sufficient reason to avoid the whole field of human suffering.

"White guilt" refers to the concept of individual or collective guilt felt by some white people for the racist treatment of black people. The term is generally used in a derogatory way. White guilt has been described as one of several psychosocial costs of racism.

At your small group meeting this week, watch the next session of the documentary feature called "Interrupted—Part II." The video segments are available for purchase on the *Interrupted* product page of *LifeWay.com*.

How do you typically respond to the field of human suffering, knowing it is plagued with Judases and weeds? How does that reality affect your involvement?

If Jesus adopted your attitude, would the cross be a happy ending or a tragic omission?

BECOMING A LOW LIFE

My daughter Sydney, 6 at the time, happened to be home when UPS delivered the package containing my first book. It came a week earlier than expected, so I was completely unprepared for book euphoria, and she was the only spectator in the "Jen Receiving Her First Book in the Mail" show. This was the culmination of so much work, the realization of a dream seeded in my heart.

I'd envisioned a scene reminiscent of *Back to the Future* when made-over George McFly opened his first novel and quipped: "Like I've always told you Marty, you put your mind to it, you can accomplish anything," while everyone looked on adoringly and Biff waxed their cars. I grabbed Sydney's hand and forced her to witness the opening of the box. And there it was. They really published it. I covered my mouth and worked up some melodramatic tears to punctuate the scene, when Sydney the Buzz Kill looked at me and asked: "What's for dinner?"

She had clearly missed the gravity of the occasion and ruined my McFly moment. Six-year-olds are unparalleled narcissists. But the disciples give them a run for their money, because not three seconds after this monumental teaching by Jesus about becoming the meal, "a dispute arose among them about who should be considered the greatest" (Luke 22:24). Unbelievable. Their insensitivity could be funny if it weren't so tragic.

I would've gone all "Gladiator" on them, but Jesus took a better approach. He chose to repeat the same point but with a fresh illustration. If the "what" was to become broken and poured out

This isn't the only place the disciples jockeyed for position in Jesus' kingdom. In Matthew 20, James and John convinced their mother to ask Jesus to give her boys a special role of authority. Jesus responded in that passage by telling them that those who want to be great must become servants.

for the restoration of hopeless humanity, then Jesus next explained the "how." This part confirmed my suspicion that brokenness was going to hurt.

> **Read Luke 22:25-30. Why do you think Jesus used the example of Benefactors rather than Pharisees? What emotion was He triggering in the disciples' hearts?**

> **What's the point He was trying to make?**

The disciples would have been familiar with the term "Benefactor," as it was a title assumed by rulers in Egypt, Syria, and Rome as a display of honor, though it had no bearing on actual service rendered to the people. Rather, these rulers were consumed with promotion and accumulation. The people they led were a means to their own end, bargaining chips for more power and prestige.

The more things change, the more they stay the same.

The Benefactors of that day were climbers. They were willing to use people in whatever way it benefited them the most. Likewise, our culture is built on ascending—up, next level, a notch higher, the top is better, top of the food chain—even in church. The pursuit of the ascent is crippling and has stunted my faith more than any other evil I've battled. It saddles us with so much to defend, and ironically, it doesn't deliver because the more we accumulate, the more fearful we become that we're just one slip from losing it all.

Consequently, my love for others is tainted because they unwittingly become articles for consumption. With every relationship, I have to ask: *How is this person making me feel better? How is she making me stronger? How is he contributing to my agenda? What can this group do for me?* I'm an addict, addicted to the ascent, positioning myself above people who can propel my upward momentum, and below those who are also longing for a higher rank and might pull me up with them. It feels desperate and frantic, and I'm so over being enslaved to the elusive top rung.

The term *benefactor* was an "honorary title bestowed on kings or other prominent people for some meritorious achievement or public service."[24]

When Jesus said, "Take the lowest place" (Luke 14:9), He was talking about more than a strategy for social justice. The path of descent is also the path to liberation. You are no longer compelled to be right and are thus relieved from the burden of maintaining some reputation. You are released from the idols of greed, control, and status. The pressure to protect your house of cards is alleviated when you take the lowest place.

What is your experience with the pursuit of the ascent?

Depending on how you answered, what has that produced in your heart?

"GET OFF YOUR HIGH HORSE" –JESUS

"But you are not to be like that," says Jesus (Luke 22:26, NIV). That's no way to live. It's no way to live for ourselves, much less for Jesus. When believers play by the rules of power, we become benefactors, using those we are charged to serve and cutting off those who no longer advance our agenda. Jesus' point was clear: *Don't get sucked into the game.* Be counter-cultural. Be the opposite of great. If that means others are ahead of you, so what? If people criticize your method or motive, what difference does it make? If you're removed from the map of recognition—good.

"If the ladder is not leaning against the right wall, every step we take just gets us to the wrong place faster."
–Stephen Covey

This is a painful decent. Reorienting our lives at the bottom involves a spiritual and mental purging of the attitudes, habits, and perspectives we learned on the way up. It's a stripping away process that leaves us raw, because in order for God's kingdom to come, our kingdoms have to go.

Has God taken you down? If so, what was the process like?

What would it practically mean for you to stop pursuing your own kingdom?

But once you hit bottom and recover somewhat from the descent, it's shockingly peaceful down there. It's much quieter. The chaos of ego and pride recedes. Releasing the compulsion to be right, to be respected, to be understood, to be winning—if not natural—is certainly relieving.

It's almost like Jesus knew that the secret of life awaits us at the bottom. At least that's what He emphasized all the time through parable and story, by example, directly and indirectly, corporately and privately. "Jesus did not seek out the rich and powerful in order to trickle down his kingdom. Rather, he joined those at the bottom, the outcasts and undesirables, and everyone was attracted to his love for people on the margins," wrote Shane Claiborne. "Then he invited everyone into a journey of downward mobility to become the least."[25]

If the kingdom of God belongs to the poor, the bottom dwellers, then rich Western Christians might have the hardest time finding it. The whole filthy engine is designed to benefit the top, and that's our zip code. Perhaps this is why the church is gaining ground in impoverished and oppressed regions but is declining in the U.S. and other affluent continents like Europe and Australia. The needy world isn't interested in God because He might secure their promotion or deliver an offer on their house in a wilting market. By the millions, the poor are running to the cross because the love of a redeeming Savior is too intoxicating to resist. Jesus is their hope and inheritance, and they glory in Him despite crushing poverty, political upheaval, and endless instability. They already live at the bottom, in Jesus' zip code.

Why do you think Jesus said it was so hard for the rich to inherit the kingdom of heaven?

Listen to "In You" by Dave Hunt from the *Interrupted* playlist. Your group leader can e-mail you the whole playlist, or you can download it for free on the *Interrupted* product page of *LifeWay.com*, under "Support Materials."

"In this life we cannot do great things. We can only do small things with great love." –Mother Teresa

To find out where you rank in the order of the world's wealthiest people, check out *globalrichlist.com*. You might be surprised.

Those in need are, in reality, so much closer to the secret of life than the privileged. I worry sometimes that it's impossible for me to truly identify with Christ, since I'm at the top of the global food chain: white, American, educated, affluent, healthy, Texan (wink). The rest of the world struggles with hunger and sickness, but I have to conquer the diseases of greed and ego, which are hard to cure in their own way.

Jesus said, "It is easier for a camel to go through the eye of a needle than for a rich person to enter the kingdom of God." I now understand that's me (Matthew 19:24). And you. The better off we are, the higher up we are, the harder it is to adopt the heart of Christ. We're farthest from the freedom that only exists at the bottom, and that's the kind of liberation money can't buy.

If you are a top dweller, what would be the most liberating thing to release if you were willing to descend?

What stops you from taking the lowest place?

GREAT

When Jesus spoke, it was the "losers" who understood while the "winners" were stumped and called Him a lunatic. You almost have to be marginalized to become capable of hearing the gospel. On the margins, as Richard Rohr explains, Jesus' social implications are crystal clear: "There we learn that we can't use Jesus to defend and maintain our position of power and wealth or to keep up for our own sake a positive self-image as polite and decent people. It could be that Jesus will lead us to a place where we ourselves don't even know whether we're holy, where all we know is that we have work to do, where we have to obey the word that we've heard in our heart."[26]

After exposing the benefactors, Jesus elaborated on the posture of a true disciple.

Read Luke 22:26. If this was the only statement out of Jesus' mouth ever recorded and you had no others, how would obedience to this command alone revolutionize your relationships (maybe pick one specifically)? Your job? Your life?

"For even the Son of Man did not come to be served, but to serve, and to give His life—a ransom for many" (Mark 10:45).

What would the church look like in the world if we were faithful to this one charge?

I get why Jesus used the word *youngest* in this passage. My 6-year-old Caleb is a loyal disciple to his older siblings. Despite his worship of them, he's always in last place. He came in the other day sobbing, "We were playing a game where we did a funny act in front of each other, and then we got scored, and Gavin and Sydney were so funny and they gave each other eights and nines, because they thought they were so awesome, but when I did my act, they only gave me half a point, because *my act is so lame!*" I assure you, Caleb is not lame (ask anyone). He is, unknowingly, the funniest kid on the planet. But by *youngest*, I think Jesus meant becoming content with half a point instead of an eight or nine. Then Jesus continued:

" . . . and whoever leads, like the one serving. For who is greater, the one at the table or the one serving?" (Luke 22:26-27).

This moment makes me laugh, because I envision a pregnant pause while the disciples tried to figure out the right response. It was rarely the obvious answer with Jesus, so I can see them staring at His mouth, watching for a consonant to form to give them a clue. "It's the one who . . . is . . . at the . . . table or serving . . . with the food . . . and the guy . . ." God bless 'em.

"Is it not the one who is at the table?" (Luke 22:27).

Make no mistake: Culture has and always will tell us the one being served is greater. The table dweller has arrived. He is our standard and goal.

SESSION TWO LOW   49

Enter Jesus:

"But I am among you as one who serves."

Jesus had already made a strong case for the descent: Become broken and poured out for others, constantly make His sacrifice real, desire with desire to do so, and resist the power politics of the benefactors. But as His closing statement, He called Himself a servant, making this worldview nearly impossible to spin or misconstrue.

Is this not why the gospel is such good news for the broken? Jesus redefined the nature of greatness, which has always rung hollow for the least and last. He took its connotation away from power and possessions and bestowed it on the humility of a servant. The more you defer? The more grateful you are to be broken and poured out? The more you choose "servant" over "benefactor"?

The greater you are.

So be it in my life, and so be it in the church. May intentional servanthood be the basis of all mission, all benevolence, all evangelism, all sacrifice. I dream of a church that is once again called great, even by our skeptics, because our works of mercy cannot be denied. I want no part in a movement that is deemed "great" because we've adopted some exceptional qualities admired by the top.

I want the church to be great because we fed hungry mommas and their babies. I'd like the church to be great because we battled poverty with not just our money but our hands and hearts. I desire the greatness that comes from not just seeking mercy but justice for those caught in a system with trap doors. I hope to be part of a great movement of the Holy Spirit, who injects supernatural wind and fire into His mission. My version of great will come when others are scratching their heads and saying: "Wow. You live a really different life."

What is your definition of "great"?

How is your life structured around that perspective?

"Justice has two major aspects.... It is the standard for both punishment and benefits and thus can be spoken of as a plumb line.... As the sovereign Creator of the universe, God is just.... Justice is also a central demand on all people who bear the name of God."[27]

BRANDON'S TAKE

"God, if You're really in this, show me, too."

I knew it was a dangerous prayer. But I meant it. While Jen was on the ride of her life, I began mine. It felt right and dangerous. I began to pray like never before. And I studied the Bible looking for one answer: "Lord, do You really want me to change the way I care, minister to, and think about others, especially the least of these?"

Throughout the spring of 2007, I had several divine encounters that were such obvious "yes, I'm in this" confirmations, they still give me chills. Here's one of them:

It was my day off. I'd been pressing heavily into God, asking Him to show me the areas in my life that needed change. That day I decided to test the waters and just be available to be a blessing, to whomever.

Leaving the house, I had the strong impression I would serve a homeless man that day. I jumped in my truck and asked God, "There are so many homeless in Austin. How will I know which one?"

God quickly responded in Spirit, "You'll know."

I drove to a used car lot to visit with an acquaintance who worked there, and while talking with him I noticed him staring over my left shoulder with a perplexed look on his face. I turned to see what had caught his attention, and I was floored: a deaf homeless man. He was staring me right in the eyes, pointing to a brand new picture of Jesus in his left hand.

I spent the day with the man. I met his wife who had cancer, shared a meal with them, and took them grocery shopping. I helped with some immediate needs at the day-rate motel they were about to get kicked out of. And never saw him again.

The rest of the story came later when I went to my office. Driving there, I added up how much it cost me that day to serve a complete stranger. It totaled $195. Still thinking about the money, I entered my office and saw an envelope with my name on it. Inside was a reimbursement I had forgotten about. The check was for $195.

God wasn't saying, "Bless others and I'll give you money"; He was saying, "The provision was not from you, it was from Me. What you have is not yours. You have a lot to learn. The first is this: You can trust Me when I call."

NOTES

INTERRUPTING YOUR LIFE

Here are some of the major influences in this part of Jen's story. To go further with some of the ideas from this session, pick one out to dig into yourself:

* "Isn't She Beautiful?" Mars Hill church conference (*marshill.org*)
* *Mother Teresa: In My Own Words* by Mother Teresa
* *My Sister, My Brother: Life Together in Christ* by Henri Nouwen and Jean Maalouf
* *Don't Waste Your Life* by John Piper

SESSION THREE
LEAST

Some parents pray for their children's future
spouses with an emphasis on certain qualities.
Evidently, traits like godliness and humility are
things to major on. This is cute and all, but in the
family I grew up in, we engaged in a different
sort of prayer. See, we are a loud and funny
tribe, and joining us is not for the faint of heart
(or the lame). Our spousal applicants *could*
demonstrate godliness and all that, but what
really separated them from inferior candidates
was how they performed on our primary King
Family Assessment: Are they funny?

My sister Cortney's selection, Zac, proved
himself a contender as he demonstrated
advanced skills in dry wit and banter. During
Zac's trial period, he secured his position as top
nominee when we saw his backyard.

HERE PRETENDING TO BE THERE

It was vintage white trash, complete with half-broken chairs and Christmas lights. Next to the well-worn dog run—you guessed it: Rottweiler alert—was a Man Grill that cost more than my car. (Zac is a competitive barbequer, which certainly didn't hurt his running tally.) Strewn around the yard were massacred remains of the trash, plus fluffy bits of shredded cushions against which the rotty waged daily war.

All this made an ideal backdrop for the crown jewel: an above ground pool with a pesky filtration system that couldn't conquer the top layer of leaves and film. But the moment we knew that Zac would, nay, *should* become ours is when we saw the hand-painted plywood sign staked into the ground: "Zacapulco."

Not only did we snatch him off the open market and claim him for ourselves, we've also since adopted his inventive use of tropical irony for our yards, complete with proper signage:

> • Brandon and Jen Hatmaker + Puerto Vallarta = "Hat-o-Vallarta"
> • Larry and Jana King + Key Largo = "King Largo"
> • Drew and Angie King + Cabo San Lucas = "Cabo San Drewcas"
> • Lindsay King + Cancun = "Kingcun"

I guess the reason we have to post signs to remind us where we are, is because we're not really at our destination. We're using the terminology and borrowing the symbolism; we're making labels and showcasing our preferences. But at the end of the day, we're still in our backyards and not in tropical paradise. We're *here* pretending to be *there*.

A frustrating trait about God is how He expects us to act on conviction fairly quickly. Pretty much the second He convinces us to move, to change, to shift, we're supposed to. Despite how much we ponder it or talk about it, until we are obedient in word and deed, we're just here pretending to be there.

As for Brandon and me, God first captured our minds, convicting us of apathy and opening our eyes to human suffering. Then He seized our hearts, instilling desire for life and service at the bottom. And quickly behind that was the call to our hands—get moving. Because as James basically said, if all we do is talk theology and pat the forsaken on the head with a hearty "Best of luck with that need!"—what good is it?

"If a brother or sister is without clothes and lacks daily food, and one of you says to them, 'Go in peace, keep warm, and eat well,' but you don't give them what the body needs, what good is it?" (James 2:15-16).

Do you have a particular struggle with one of these handoffs: Mind to heart? Heart to hands?

Why do you think you get stalled?

DON'T KNOW IF WE'RE COMING OR GOING

Mind. Heart. Hands. That's the progression.

In theory? Doable. In practice? Paralysis. In our context, we had no idea what to do with our lives, much less in church. We were familiar with an attractional model of church, which is somewhat successful if the target audience actually wants to go to church. "Build it and they will come" works for those who want a building and feel like coming to it.

But these people?

These people included those in physical, emotional, and financial crisis. But if "they" had to come to "us" for a human touch, this left us in the lurch. What about the really broken people who can't or won't find their way to us? What about those too frozen in suffering to consider a 9:30 or 11 a.m. service? And also, what about the people who despise church and Christians and can't for the life of them figure out what is "good" about our Good News? What about the spiritually hungry who keep leaving churches uninspired and unmoved?

Who is your "they"?

"No one who puts his hand to the plow and looks back is fit for the kingdom of God" (Luke 9:62).

Do you think most people who aren't going to church are interested in coming to church? Why or why not?

For more stats on these and similar issues, read the full articles at *lifewayresearch.com* and *barna.org*.

George Barna's book, *Revolution*, is a short but challenging read. In it, Barna discusses current trends in church attendance and how the church must change in order to adapt to the changing nature of spirituality.

This raises a question: Are *they* coming to us? Lots of them aren't. Statistics like these are causing millions of believers to rethink an attractional model of church that isn't attracting people like it used to:

* Only 3 out of 10 people in their 20s attend church in a typical week, compared to 4 out of 10 people in their 30s, and 5 out of 10 in their 40s and older.[28]

* While that sounds like a small decline, that 3 out of 10 instead of a 4 or 5 out of 10 represents millions of young adults rejecting the organized church. If the trend holds, the church is two or three generations away from mass cultural irrelevance.

* Thirty-four percent of the U.S. adult population has not attended any type of church service or activity (other than weddings or funerals) during the past six months; about 73 million adults.

* Roughly 62 percent of all unchurched adults were formerly churched.[29] Let that sink in. Not only can we not draw new people, we can't keep the ones we have.

* Approximately half of all American churches did not add one new person through conversion growth last year.[30]

* More than 80 percent of the current growth registered by Protestant churches is biological or transfer growth; meaning new children are born into the church or believers are church hopping.[31] We're not adding to the kingdom—we're simply reshuffling the deck.

* In America, it takes the combined efforts of 85 Christians working over an entire year to produce one convert.[32]

* In a nationwide survey, 94 percent of churches were either not growing or losing ground in the communities they serve.[33]

* Thom Rainer and his research team predict that 50,000 churches will close by 2010; roughly one in every eight.[34]

I know statistics can say anything, and wading through these left me grouchy and fuzzy, but no matter how you slice it, millions of Christians have left the organized church in the last 20 years, and we're not drawing the next generation. The trend is clearly downward, and at this pace, reimagining church is not just the task of mavericks; it's for the survival of the whole bride.

How do these statistics square up with your experience? What are you seeing in your community?

What do you think is repelling the next generation from church?

At your small group meeting this week, watch part three of the documentary feature called "Interrupted—Part III." The video segments are available for purchase on the *Interrupted* product page of *LifeWay.com*.

The world is increasingly uninterested in our Christian story. Its current presentation just isn't compelling. Most believers who represent Christianity battle boredom and apathy; they are spiritually immature and demonstrate religiosity without transformation. Our faith communities run the gamut from judgmental high church to feel-good talent shows, and people aren't buying it anymore. Remarkably, most outsiders are not anti-church (our gospel isn't provocative enough to incite backlash anymore). They simply dismiss the church as irrelevant to their real lives, since it seems mostly irrelevant to the people who go there.

Lost in America will motivate Christians, individually and in the church, to think and behave as missionaries right here in North America. The case is made that the church has become marginalized in our society and requires changes to make it relevant in reaching our highly relational, postmodern society. *Lost in America* helps Christians re-image their church as a mission station and shows them how they can meaningfully offer hope to the unchurched in America.

"Christianity has lost its place as the center of American life," wrote Tom Clegg and Warren Bird in *Lost in America*. "Christians must learn how to live the gospel as a distinct people who no longer occupy the center of society. We must learn to build relational bridges that win a hearing."[35] Our Christian rhetoric has become white noise, I'm afraid. It gets hopelessly stuck in our minds and struggles to transition to our hearts and then hands.

Our only hope is to follow the example of Jesus and get back out there, winning people over with ridiculous love and a lifestyle that causes them to finally sit up and take notice. Listen, no church can ever do this for me. This is my high calling to live on mission as an adopted daughter of God. If people around me aren't moved by my Christ or my church, then I must be doing a miserable job of representing them both.

Written for those who are trying to nurture authentic faith communities and for those who have struggled to retain their faith, *The Tangible Kingdom* offers theological answers and real-life stories that demonstrate how the best ancient church practices can re-emerge in today's culture in any size church. Learn more at *missio.us.*

"Change must be about *new,* which to us means 'fresh, bright, something that intuitively feels right, that causes us not only to dream but to move on our dreams,'" write Hugh Halter and Matt Smay in *The Tangible Kingdom.* They go on: "That kind of new is good if it compels us into a world of faith again where we can battle fear and despondency with action that makes a difference. That kind of new is okay, but it really isn't new. It's just been hidden, or covered, or we've been distracted from it.

"This type of new is about a returning. Returning to something ancient, something tried, something true and trustworthy. Something that has rerouted the legacies of families, nations, kings, and peasants. Something that has caused hundreds of thousands to give up security, reputation, and their lives. What we need to dig up, recover, and find again is the life of the kingdom and Jesus' community … the church. It's not anti-church; it's pro-church. It's about the type of church that Jesus would go to, the type he died to give flight to."[36]

> **What type of church would you expect to find Jesus in if He lived on earth today?**

> **What type of church would He have harsh words for?**

JUSTICE FOR JESUS

I am being lured back to the way of the Spirit. He is the fresh wind everyone is looking for. He reminds me I am a member of a grand assembly that inspires and stirs and empowers. On bad days, when I secretly whisper, "Is this all there is?", it is the Spirit who urges me to join Him at the bottom, where the best grassroots movements have always begun.

He is the *new* I was craving when I realized my heart was dry.

Paul explained that we "serve in the new way of the Spirit" (Romans 7:6). That's a nice thought, but what does it mean? How are we to serve in a new way of the Spirit? And if that service involves *us going* instead of *them coming*, we have to leave our safety zones where we know the religious rules and get out there where those rules don't apply. I, for one, am still figuring out what that means. So I started asking God. Cut to Matthew 25:31-46, a passage I had never in my life taken seriously.

Read Matthew 25:31-46. What's your initial response to this passage?

Listen to "All Because of Your Love" by Kate Hurley from the *Interrupted* playlist. Your group leader can e-mail you the whole playlist, or you can download it for free on the *Interrupted* product page of *LifeWay.com*, under "Support Materials."

What do you like about it? What bothers you?

It begins with Jesus describing this final drama:

"When the Son of Man comes in His glory, and all the angels with Him, then He will sit on the throne of His glory. All the nations will be gathered before Him."

Having endured sermonizing my entire childhood on Judgment Day and the Four Horse Apocalypse, I took something of a sabbatical from the topic as an adult.

But after clearing the legalistic static, now I see two perspectives that bring me comfort instead of turn-or-burn fear. The first is the basic foreknowledge that Jesus will get His just due. The dishonor heaped on Christ when He walked the earth has always assaulted my sense of justice, leaving me raw and unsettled. The silent, will-not-defend-myself posture Jesus maintained fries a circuit in my brain. I have always needed closure on the sins committed against Jesus.

"Judgment Day" is the day in the future when God will judge both the wicked and the righteous. Read more about the events in Revelation 20:10-15.

"He will sit on the throne of His glory" does the trick nicely. I feel such relief when I read about Jesus' eternal glory. All is set right in my world; I don't have to accept the injustice He accepted. One day all His haters and critics and doubters and mockers will be unable to hate and criticize and doubt and mock, because Jesus will come in full glory, the glory that belongs to Him alone, the glory He earned and deserves. Justice will be suspended no longer, and the King will get the worship He is owed. I realize Jesus reigned on the cross in humiliation, but I'm ready for Him to reign on the throne in glory. That is where my Jesus belongs. Until then, He waits patiently at the right hand of God, delaying His fame for the sake of one more believer, two more, three more. . . .

His sacrifice for us continues.

Are you motivated by Jesus' glory?

Your answer is actually central to the way you live. Think of what plagues your spiritual life most. Do you see a link?

This brings me to my second thought: My children are elementary aged, so the worst school behavior we've faced involved my fifth grader making sarcastic comments at inappropriate moments (don't say it). But we are four years from high school, where things could get dicey. I fully expect my kids to be perfect, never mouth off, always turn in their AP work, and salvage their teachers' hope for the next generation. I daresay awards will be created to honor their impeccable behavior, given the extremely compliant DNA they were blessed with from model parents. However, should the bad kids negatively influence my good kids toward shenanigans (I'm planning to play that card), I have an ace up my sleeve, a little weapon I intend to use liberally and without reservation: My mom is the high school principal.

I'm not saying she should give them preferential treatment and strategically place them with the best teachers (that is exactly what I'm saying), but there is comfort in knowing that if something goes wrong, if something heads south, if my kids end up facing the music, Principal King is also known as Grana. They will find mercy because they are her babies, and blood runs thick.

Ⓡ

Check out Max Lucado's *In the Grip of Grace* for a picture of the mercy and friendship God offers.

"At the name of Jesus every knee should bow—of those who are in heaven and on earth and under the earth—and every tongue should confess that Jesus Christ is Lord, to the glory of God the Father" (Philippians 2:10-11).

As I read Matthew 25 with Jesus as Judge, it is something akin to having your Grana double as your principal. No one loves me more than Jesus. No one is more on my side. No one is more obsessed with His sons and daughters. No one else laid down His life to defend me. It's walking into court and finding out your best friend is hearing the case. If Jesus as Judge used to scare me, now it comforts me, because "no condemnation now exists for those in Christ Jesus" (Romans 8:1). The Judge also goes by the name Friend. His justice is constructed on mercy, and I'll never stand before a judge more hell-bent on my liberation.

If you've played out this final scenario in your mind, what happens?

Do you imagine Jesus leading with judgment or grace? Why?

A WORD ABOUT FARM ANIMALS

But Jesus does paint a picture of a trial of sorts, and the issue at hand is pretty simple. It's not a very complex case; there aren't a lot of gray areas. Jesus is like that: two roads, two masters, two commandments, two sons, two houses.

How did Jesus separate the sheep from the goats?

Does the sheep and goat metaphor contradict any of your notions about the final judgment?

The metaphor of the sheep and the goat runs throughout the Bible. In the Old and New Testament, the people of God are frequently referred to as sheep (see Psalm 23, John 10, and Luke 15 for some examples). The goat appears as well, most notably in Leviticus 16, where the priests were instructed to symbolically release a goat into the wilderness as representative of the sin of the people being sent away.

"If we should deal out justice only, in this world, who would escape? No, it is better to be generous, and in the end more profitable, for it gains gratitude for us, and love." –Mark Twain

Jesus was in the midst of teaching the disciples kingdom priorities. This was His final week. He knew it; they didn't. Much like a terminally ill patient speaks the most important words when death is near, Jesus taught with urgency and priority. The disciples had pressed Him for clarification on the end of the age, so Jesus explained a series of parables to help them wrap their minds around it.

Be like the wise, watchful servant, not the wicked, abusive one. Emulate the five wise virgins, not the foolish, sleepy ones. Act like the servant with five invested talents, not the frightened servant with one buried talent. And as Jesus built His case, and the disciples began to gauge what counted and what wouldn't, He hit them with the grand finale: It will only matter if you're a sheep or a goat—the blessed and lost will be separated based on the care of the forsaken. The end.

The finest communicator to ever grace this planet, Jesus plays the role of Judge and King; the only instance, in fact, when He gave Himself that title. He drew Himself up to full stature; all the power, all the position, all the authority He would willingly defer later that week. He was King Supreme, and He alone would be sifting the wheat from the chaff. And in that paradoxical way of His, Jesus threw all His weight behind those at the very bottom of the pile. Last will be first; blessed are the poor; proud will be leveled. His highest rank on behalf of the lowest class.

What are three changes the church needs to make to more effectively communicate Jesus' "last will be first" and "blessed are the poor" truths to the world?

LAST BUT NOT LEAST

Hungry. Thirsty. Lonely. Naked. Sick. Imprisoned. The messy reality of suffering is mentioned not once, not twice, but four times throughout this short parable. It's worth repeating, because although we've heard these words so often that they seem ordinary, they are actually some of the most revolutionary claims ever made. Immediately before the narrative of Jesus' passion and death, He presents the scene of the last judgment as a strategic metaphor wherein the least human person is identified with the Lord of history.

This parable is an indictment on humanity's violent resistance to God's revelation of the dignity of every human life. In only the last century, millions have been killed in the Middle East for the sake of homeland and nation. Six million Jews were systematically murdered during the horror of the Holocaust. Eleven million Hindus and Muslims were slaughtered at the dawn of Indian independence. Twenty million were massacred in the purging of Communist China. Rwanda, Serbia, Darfur—all sank under the tidal wave of genocide. Men, women, and children of every color, tribe, race, and creed were bound, traded, and killed upon birth, such was their disvalue.

Away from the fields of war, unborn babies are destroyed in their mothers' wombs under the umbrella of preference. Seniors are cast aside in their twilight years, a ballast on our ambitions. Our teens learn to kill with their words, repeating patterns they've learned from Hollywood and home. Our veterans sleep under bridges, forever damaged by trauma and neglect. The cycles of poverty churn out unparented children who act out with violence and confusion.

What are some other examples you can think of that devalue human life?

Which of these hit you hardest? Why?

The Book of Genesis states that God created humans in His own image (Genesis 1:26). There is debate surrounding the implications of what that entails. Some argue that being created in God's image gives us the ability to think rationally. Others claim it is defined in our ability to rule over creation. What everyone agrees on is that being made in the image of God requires us to recognize the dignity and preciousness of every human life.

To such a bleak history, the King cries, "As often as you have done this to the least of these brothers and sisters of mine, you have done it to me." In the scope of human bedlam, we have maimed the body of Christ. The starving, the unwanted old and unborn, the criminal, those of wrong color, ideology, sex, nation, class—whatever category renders a person *least* in our minds—bear the face of Jesus.

Do you see Jesus in the faces of the least or not? If not, what do you see in their faces instead?

If you do, what has He taught you about Himself through their stories?

It's so mad and overwhelming, Christians pretend not to hear it.

Or instead of selective hearing, there is some spiritual two-stepping involved to get out of the implications of this text as well. A couple of interpretations exist wherein this scenario is simply a slice of what to expect during the Great Tribulation after you and I are safely raptured. Conveniently, this means we don't have to worry our little heads with the whole sheep or goat dilemma. So if you adhere to that dispensational interpretation, feel free to skip the next few paragraphs until I'm done ranting.

Of course, there is also the explanation posed by many scholars that these brothers and sisters of Jesus' refer mainly to suffering believers and perhaps secondarily to all humanity, if at all. This reading is largely based on the habit Jesus made of calling believers "brothers" in the gospel of Matthew. If this is your position, let me say that if you want to start with the poor, sick, hungry, imprisoned believers of the world, then you'll have plenty to do, so go right ahead. Indeed, we have millions of impoverished brothers and sisters in Christ both at home and abroad, so that will certainly keep you busy. That is a noble and necessary task.

As for me, I'm going to gamble on the fact that Jesus didn't have much patience with believers who attempted to limit the scope of 'who my neighbor is' to the fewest possible people. Jesus always fell left of center here, extending grace and healing to those well outside His party lines. He often healed people first—they believed second. If I'm wrong, the worst thing that could happen is that some desperate people were cared for, and I'm guessing Jesus will look the other way.

The Great Tribulation is described in the Bible as a period of time in the future when the world will suffer calamities and destruction prior to the second coming of Christ (Daniel 12; Matthew 24:15-22; Revelation 2:22; 7:14). The time and nature of the Great Tribulation is one of the most debated issues in Christian theology.

He favors unmerited grace. To me, this is a wheat and weeds issue, and since that's not my call to make, I'll just err on the side of mercy and let Jesus sort it out at the harvest.

Read Luke 10:25-37. What's the main point of Jesus' teaching in this passage?

How does that relate to the parable in Matthew 25?

Jesus was intentionally shocking in His choice of the Samaritan to be the hero in this story. The Samaritans were looked down on by the Jewish people, seen as "half-breeds" and religious encroachers. By choosing a Samaritan as the hero, Jesus was further emphasizing His commitment that the gospel go out to everyone in every culture.

Jesus' identification with the least is the cornerstone of the parable in Matthew 25. He tells of the day when the righteous will stand before Him, surprised at the credit they're receiving for caring. In fact, some people believe this parable teaches that even people who didn't know Jesus and certainly were not motivated by His kingdom will be welcomed as righteous simply for their attention to the least.

While my soft side loves that concept, I don't buy it. Many will stand before Jesus one day clutching good works in their hands, but they will leave His presence because they never really loved Him. If we've learned anything from the rebellious nation of Israel, the Pharisees and Sadducees, and the meager offerings of the poor in Scripture, it is this: God is supremely concerned with our motives, and our works only count when they match our intentions. There is no back door into salvation, rerouted around the sacrifice of Christ. Otherwise, the whole earth could gain heaven by good works, and His day on the cross was pointless.

Jesus was describing the moment when His followers, His beloved sons and daughters, will stand before Him: "Of course we loved the poor, Jesus. You told us to. Of course we opened our homes and invited the lonely in. That was clear in the Word. Of course we clothed naked children and fed starving people. They are human beings made in Your image. We took care of the least in obedience to You, Jesus, but we never had the privilege of actually serving You. We did all that *for* You." But Jesus will say: "No, you did that *unto* Me."

Check out the video clip "Walking Across Egypt: Cake to Jesus" on *wingclips.com* to have a look at an example of stepping outside the routine to serve the least.

That's the shocker. It's not surprising that we adopt His bias toward the bottom, and He is pleased. It's startling that He is actually served. We clearly don't comprehend how personally Jesus takes it when we love justice. He is so utterly identified with the afflicted that there is nothing more obedient, more pleasing, or more central than serving the marginalized.

We have the privilege of serving Jesus Himself every time we feed a hungry belly, each moment we give dignity to someone who has none left, when we acknowledge the value of a convict because he is a human being, when we share our extreme excess with those who have nothing, when we love the forsaken and remember the forgotten. Jesus is there.

Have you ever had a divine encounter with Jesus in the least? What was that experience like?

POOR PEOPLE

If we want to find where Jesus is and go there, the only option is a stumbling, awkward journey downward. And it is awkward. However, as Franciscan priest Richard Rohr observed, "We cannot think our way into a new kind of living. We must live our way into a new kind of thinking." (His book, *Simplicity*, is so brilliant and profound, I find myself wanting to plagiarize the entire thing.)

When I consider what the Mother Theresas and the John Hayeses have done, I kind of want to laugh out loud and/or cry at my own ridiculous foray into the world of poverty. My family isn't a bunch of revolutionaries—I'm in the PTA, for Pete's sake. It's beyond humbling—it's embarrassing to admit that the saints have quietly done this work for centuries and continue to do it today, with little or no recognition. I am not leading the charge; I'm scrambling behind it trying to catch up. I am more aware of my own poverty and smallness than ever, so don't imagine for a moment that this is a source of reverse spiritual pride.

But every new season begins somewhere small, and so my family turned our eyes to the poor. This involved lots of time downtown feeding the hungry, picking up men with no legs (ask my kids about

Serving the least is more at our fingertips than ever before. Check out these Web sites to find out how you can sponsor a child and change a life forever:
• *compassion.com*;
• *worldvision.org*;
• *childfund.org*.

National Coalition for the Homeless estimates that in the U.S. roughly one percent of the population is homeless (about 3.5 million), 39 percent of them children.

this) and taking them and others like them to dinner, transforming Valentine's Day into a family excursion to the darkest underbelly of Austin—stuff like that. We changed the way we celebrated holidays, attempting to filter them through the gospel instead of culture. We latched on to the informed and active, soaking up their knowledge and experience like sponges. Painfully, we overhauled our personal budget, freeing up some excess to share. We began chipping away at the walls we'd constructed between "us" and "them," and discovered common ground instead.

What is the next major holiday coming up? How could you celebrate it in a manner worthy of the gospel, even if that has no resemblance to the way our culture enjoys it?

When believers accustomed to privilege start moving downward toward "poor people," we inevitably demonstrate an "us" and "them" mentality. We typically place more emphasis on their status as "poor" than the superior label: "people." But Jesus calls us beyond that. When they were "poor" to me, then I was the benevolent, hyper-friendly white girl who had a hard time entering into a real conversation. The emphasis was on what I was offering: food, gloves, water, a bus pass.

This is an OK place to start, but here is where that "you did it for Me" thing comes in. You start noticing their need less and less and their humanity more and more. You realize these are daddies and sisters and lost sons and daughters. They have stories and dreams. Their wallets are full of pictures, and their histories are full of heartache. They are funny and wildly talented (Johnny the Bucket Drummer played at our church once—brought down the house).

I found that out as we looked each other in the eyes, and we were the same. We're all poor; I just have more stuff. Just fragile humans who are patterned after Jesus, which makes us all beautiful. Amazingly, as we start to identify with the least, and Jesus acknowledged that He was the least, we start to commune with Christ Himself at the bottom in a new, earnest way.

The book *Under the Overpass* is the story of Mike Yankoski, a Christian college student who chose to live as a homeless person in six American cities for five months. His account is a challenge to learn about faith, identify with the poor, and find "more forgotten, ruined, beautiful people than we ever imagined existed, and more reason to hope in their redemption."

The Soloist (2009) is a movie based on the true story of *L.A. Times* columnist Steve Lopez's friendship with Nathaniel Ayers, a homeless, schizophrenic classical musician. The movie gives a face and a life story to the homeless community.

How would you describe your communion with Jesus?

How does your answer relate to your relationships with the forsaken?

NEW

When you start this downward transformation, you engage the seriousness of Christ's commands in stages. You start with recognition. Then you give. Then you go. Then you move. It's a progression, and that progression has to start somewhere. When you are first interrupted, God is gracious by not saddling you with the final destination before you're ready to handle it. But you *will* end up somewhere. Ignoring this call is not an option. Jesus already hammered that excuse in the sheep and goats story:

Re-read Matthew 25:41-45. Is any one need mentioned easy for you to meet?

How about totally uncomfortable? Why?

Pastor and author Mark Batterson is committed to helping people understand that the Christian life is about more than just stopping the bad things that we do. In his Threads study, *Chase the Lion*, Batterson argues that the real spiritual adventure begins when we start taking chances and reducing our sins of omission. Find out more at *threadsmedia.com*.

Never once did Jesus charge the goats with something they did wrong. His entire indictment was on what they didn't do right. It was a sin of neglect; a crime of omission. And it went far beyond ignoring poverty.

Jesus explained that when we ignore the least, we ignore Him. No amount of spinning or clever justification can neutralize Jesus' point. If we claim affinity for Christ but turn a blind eye to those He identified Himself with, there is no honor in that. There is no truth in it.

This is how grave the gospel's challenge is. It's as simple as it is radical. If every believer obeyed accordingly, I daresay we would become the answer to all that ails society. "Whatever you did for one of the least of these brothers of Mine, you did for Me."

These are the words by which we are sent, but wondrously, they are also the words by which we are saved. These words aren't simply a revelation of crisis and the call to active love; they are also an invitation to personal recognition. Each one of us, as it turns out, counts as the least. We all bear the image of Christ, no matter how devalued we feel. As Gerard Manley Hopkins wrote, "Christ plays in ten thousand places, lovely in limbs and lovely in eyes not his."[37]

Ultimately, it is not nation or race, church or citizenship that gives people value. It is not sinlessness or innocence that makes us precious. It is not that Jesus looks on us as helpless or powerful, poor or rich, weak or strong. We are loved because we are living images of God, made in His likeness and created for the heights of His glory and the depths of communion. Our very God took on our form for the love of humanity, privilege or poverty aside. In contrast to God's perfection, we are all the least, each and every one, identified entirely with a Savior who loves us recklessly. This parable reveals as much about the character of God as it does about the course of human affairs.

Miraculously, there will come a day when we stand before God Almighty, with nothing but this human life standing up on our behalf, full of failure and omissions. And just when all hope is lost, when we have nothing left to hold out, to show God, no more to demonstrate our worthiness with, the Son will step in, in all His glory and righteousness, and say to the Father:

"Whatever you do to the least of these, these brothers and sisters of Mine, you do unto Me."

So this Matthew 25 passage—in its greatest depth—is not merely a moral challenge or judgment on this world. Nor is it just a program for social action or poverty reduction. Rather, it describes the mystery of salvation that grounds all hierarchy, motivates all action, and makes possible our acceptance of our identity as redeemed sinners.

This quote is from Gerard Manley Hopkins' poem, "As Kingfishers Catch Fire." Read the poem in its entirety at *bartleby.com*.

Resisting the urge to plagiarize, I'll quote Rohr one last time:

"The Gospels say very clearly that God loves imperfect things. But it's only the imperfect and the broken who can believe that. Those who don't have anything to prove or protect can believe that they are loved as they are. But we who have spent our lives ascending the spiritual ladder have a harder time hearing the truth. For the truth isn't found up at the top, but down at the bottom. And by trying to climb the ladder we miss Christ, who comes down through the Incarnation."[38]

"For the bread of God is the One who comes down from heaven and gives life to the world" (John 6:33).

You are Jesus' "least of these"; He is utterly identified with you and obsessed with your restoration. What does it mean to you to be the least of these?

How does really believing that change the way you live?

BRANDON'S TAKE

It was Easter Sunday 2007, and Jen and I were worshiping with a small Asian American church in downtown Austin that was hosting guest speaker Shane Claiborne, who we were anxious to hear. In the middle of a song, I had a vision. I saw myself walking down the west campus street just outside the church we were in and a homeless guy yelled from the sidewalk, "Hey, give me your boots."

My immediate response was, "They won't fit you!" To which he replied, "Oh, they'll fit." I was confused. "Am I supposed to walk down Guadalupe Street after the service? Am I gonna see this guy? Whatever it is, God, I'll do it."

It was settled. Afterward, I would walk down the street, find that guy, and hand over my boots. But instead, I was handed a chance to obey it. In church. Not only did Shane inspire us as expected, but he also asked us to leave our socks and shoes for the homeless community at the altar, right next to the communion table, giving us an opportunity to "constantly make this real." After church, a beautiful group of believers walked outside, barefooted. I was overwhelmed. I guess that homeless guy was right. They'll fit someone.

This was for real. So we began the journey of figuring out what it looked like. The experiences were reshaping my heart, and I was being transformed. The challenge would surely be to get other Christ-followers to take the focus off themselves and place it on others, specifically on the least of these.

But something was missing. As I met with my leaders and cast the vision, it was obvious our zeal was not the same. It wasn't falling on entirely deaf ears; it just seemed to lack substance. My leadership seemed so void of His presence that I found myself literally weeping, asking God, "What am I doing wrong? Why is this not taking root? What do You want me to do?"

Then the answer came: "Brandon, this vision is not for here. There's already a vision here. I'm giving you a new one."

Over the next few weeks, God affirmed His calling to leave all that I had known. I hoped that He'd explain how that calling would manifest before we stepped away. But He was silent. That summer I discovered the journey was not only about something new, but also about being willing to go, even before we knew where we were going.

Only one thing was clear: God was calling us to a barefooted church.

NOTES

INTERRUPTING YOUR LIFE

Here are some of the major influences in this part of Jen's story. To go further with some of the ideas from this session, pick one out to dig into yourself:

* Austin Resource Center for the Homeless (*frontsteps.org*)
* The Barna Group (*barna.org*)
* *Boiling Point* by George Barna
* *Same Kind of Different as Me* by Ron Hall and Denver Moore

SESSION FOUR
FAST

Brandon and I recently hit our 15th anniversary. We rewarded our longevity with an anniversary cruise to Alaska, and made the brilliant decision to take our best friends and leave behind the children. Coincidentally, we received the unexpected reward of being labeled "the young people" on the ship, which was infinitely superior to competing with spring breakers in bikinis in Jamaica.

As an excursion, the six of us booked a zipline course through the rainforest in Ketchikan. On the waiver was this condition to consider: "Minimum weight is 90 pounds for the Rainforest Canopy and Zipline Expedition and maximum weight is 250. Weight limits are established to ensure proper zipping speed on the courses."

If you can't get to Alaska anytime soon, watch a helmet cam video for a taste of the Ketchikan Zipline Expedition at *alaskacanopy.com*.

OFF THE PLATFORM

We were all within these boundaries except for our friend Tray, proud former offensive lineman for the Alabama Crimson Tide, standing 6 feet, 4 inches, and comfortably north of the 250-pound mark. We read the fine print to determine if fudging his numbers would simply result in increased velocity or something more serious like his tragic death plunging to the rainforest floor. Hoping for the former, his wife Jenny "confirmed" the necessary weight requirements on the waiver.

As it turned out, the zipline was a little scary.

We were 135 feet up in the trees, where our zipline platforms were secured with duct tape and hot glue. All of us, including our 24-year-old guide Chad, were to zip from one platform to the next, harnessed in by skinny little ribbons and a silver buckle or two.

"Sit back into your harness and drop off the edge of the platform," instructed Chad nonchalantly, as if we were two feet off the ground. "It is your responsibility to slow down by pulling on the cable as you approach the next platform." That we were somehow responsible for our own well-being seemed fairly ridiculous, and we felt certain one of us would be dead before nightfall.

Here is when we discovered the meaning of the phrase: "Weight limits are established to ensure proper zipping speed on the courses." As we reached the 850-foot-long "Ben's Revenge," the longest and steepest zipline of the course, our lying ways caught up to us. Tray, acting on intuition and a basic understanding of physics, said, "This feels like a bad idea." He stood there for some time, as we all did, not wanting him to die but certainly willing to sacrifice him rather than perish in the treetops waiting.

Chad hollered from the next platform, where he stood ready to receive each adventurer: "Come on Tray!" So without further ado, Tray dropped off that platform and promptly turned into a speeding freight train, his "zipping speed" no longer ensured or proper. His momentum was so alarming, that from about the 300-foot mark, Chad started cussing. The closer Tray got, the lower Chad got, attempting a lineman's stance to break a landing that surely became legendary in the state of Alaska.

When Tray hit that platform with the velocity of a large speeding bullet, he knocked down the landing stairs like they were matchsticks and flattened poor, undersized Chad against the tree like a panini sandwich. Trying to be helpful, the rest of us fell down on the platform and screamed with laughter for 20 minutes. Chad earned his paycheck that day, which I'm sure he used on his cracked ribs.

The point is that leaving the platform is hard, even when a great adventure awaits you.

Our lives were interrupted, and we knew we had to leave the suburban, American Dream lifestyle we had so carefully crafted. But go where? That was somewhere out there, to be determined. What lay in front of us was the telling, the transition, leaving the platform.

Do you have a platform to leave? An adventure to engage? What is it?

What stops you from taking the leap?

For us, it was essential that our dream of becoming a missional church was primary, and how that materialized was a distant second. Otherwise, we would've held too tightly to the method, the details, the strategy. Had we become enmeshed with our specific task, there would've been much cause to doubt it in this early season. We were unprepared for the opposition and angst, and had we possessed a clear vision, we would've defiled with defensiveness something God intended to be pure.

We can wreck the Spirit of a mission by becoming prematurely focused on the strategy of the mission. When the *how* eclipses the *why* too soon, we create a positional shift to defend and execute rather than listen and receive. Once clear territory is staked, we turn into guards, protecting our decisions.

Does faith come naturally to you, or are you a planner who prefers details before obedience?

Is God holding out His vision for you in some area? If so, what might He be trying to accomplish?

The Gospels tell about a young ruler who came face to face with the opportunity to abandon his reputation, perception, position, and control. The man was encouraged by Jesus to sell everything he had and give it to the poor. With no more ties to the life he'd created for himself, the man would be free to follow Jesus without any distractions. But instead of permanently relocating to become a follower of Jesus, the man returned to his life, saddened by the circumstance (Luke 18:18-23).

Turning loose and letting God be God requires conscious decisions to abandon formerly vital things like reputation, perception, position, and control. This is especially true when you're trying to move "down" and relinquish your rank. When you just visit the bottom through an occasional service day or mission trip, you're assured that your real life is safely secured higher up. You have somewhere to go back to. But simply visiting the bottom is just charity and requires only a moment— not a permanent relocation.

It is something entirely different to adopt the mind of Christ that exists uniquely in the least. That's when you don't just act lowly; you are lowly. Your mind is not safely secured up higher, awaiting your return after you're done patronizing those at the bottom.

What do you think is the practical difference between acting lowly and being lowly?

Why would God prefer the latter?

How do you treat people at the bottom differently in each case?

The decisions you make from a low position are completely opposite those you'd make from a high place. This was probably why it wasn't until we were lying on the ground that God delivered our task and vision. When we had nothing left to protect, no position left to defend, no reputation left to guard, and no one else to please, we got our marching orders.

FREE

Our mission was to start a new church in our beloved city—roughly 93 percent unchurched or dechurched—from scratch. We didn't have a dime, a supporter, a mentor, or a plan. This was the moment in our journey of interruption when God finally stepped into the story with "The Plan."

One of the most encouraging things we found was that we were not alone. We found an entire network in the city of like-minded church-planters. We learned from leaders across denominational lines. We formed partners with other organizations and churches. And we found that some of our new friends had already articulated what was bubbling up inside us.

Within two weeks of our departure, we were contacted by an extraordinary leader from a denomination we had never heard of: the Free Methodist Church, which split from the main Methodist conference in 1860 over racial equality and the nasty habit churches had adopted of charging congregants for preferred seating in church. Convinced that both people and church attendance should be *free*, the Free Methodist Church was born.

Their target demographic was explained in *The Earnest Christian* in 1860: "At times they are tremblingly alive to the fact that a religion of fashion and parade, of pomp and show, and circumstance, cannot save their soul. The Holy Ghost presses home the truth that Christ's disciples are characterized by self-denial, humility, and love. It is for this increasing class of persons that we write."

The Free Methodist Church was founded in 1860 with a commitment to missions and racial equality that was uncommon at that time. Early on, Free Methodists were often found in black and mixed congregations, on mission fields, and in rescue missions in cities across the U.S. The Free Methodist Church continues to be recognized for a call to holy living that emphasizes not only personal piety but also redemptive action within society. Learn more at *freemethodistchurch.org*.

Their mission included one other primary group: "The claims of the neglected poor, the class to which Christ and the Apostles belonged, the class for whose special benefit the gospel was designed, to all the ordinances of Christianity, will be advocated with all the candor and ability we can command. In order that the masses, who have a peculiar claim to the Gospel of Christ may be reached, the necessity of plain churches, with the seats free, of plainness of dress, of spirituality and simplicity in worship, will, we trust, be set forth with convincing arguments."[39]

To this day, the Free Methodist churches, by their posture and passions, attract two types of people: believers hungry for the straight-up gospel—simple in presentation, powerful in expression—and the marginalized who need good news in the form of salvation, assistance, and Christian fellowship. This has always been their particular limb in the body of Christ; an extremity perhaps, but no less essential than the more conspicuous parts. It's the limb of the bare feet, and with humility and gratitude, we joined the mission they had so clearly articulated.

In evaluating your own desire to be a part of church, what's most important to you? Why?

Is that what should be most important?

ISAIAH AND ME

Now that we had the skeleton of our mission, it was time to hang some meat on the bones. I was reminded of my friend Stephanie who teaches first grade at an affluent school in Austin. During the first week of classes, a concerned father cornered her and asked, "What are you doing to prepare my son for Yale?" Quick on her feet and not in the mood for intimidation, Stephanie answered, "Well, first I'm going to teach him to stop picking his nose and eating the plunder. Next on the list is walking in a straight line for more than five seconds. I'll be ready to write a recommendation to Yale by the end of the year, I'm sure."

When you're 6, fixating on Yale is somewhat premature. When your church is eight seconds old, fancy things like services and tithe checks remain somewhere in Futureland, too. Much work is required to prep the surface, and it wasn't long before we realized we had no idea how to start a church from scratch. What do we do first? How do we stay true to the vision? It was overwhelming to jump off the platform. Studying Isaiah with several women from our core team, one particular passage became incredibly meaningful for me during those days.

Isaiah is a book of crazy contrasts. On the one hand, you have God angrily judging His people for their centuries of idolatry. But on the other hand, you have Him promising incredible restoration. You have God crying out against and on behalf of His people. And you have the people claiming to be very dedicated and yet entirely missing the point.

Read Isaiah 58:1-3. What strange dichotomy do you see between the Israelites' motives and actions?

What does this tell you about good intentions?

Have you ever felt like you were doing everything right, but God was silent? When?

If you looked deeper, was there a contradiction between your sincere motive to hear from God and the way you were actually living?

In Isaiah 58:3, the Israelites questioned why God wasn't blessing them even though they were doing what He told them, namely fasting and humbling themselves. God responded by getting at the attitude and intention behind their works. Isaiah reveals that "they fasted but did not demonstrate the attitudes and activities that fasting represented. They did not really sacrifice their own desires, and they continued to treat other people inconsiderately.... They were practicing religious ritual to try to manipulate God into blessing them."[40]

"Search me, God, and know my heart; test me and know my concerns. See if there is any offensive way in me; lead me in the everlasting way" (Psalm 139:23-24).

The point is clear: The Israelites took great pride in their religious actions while their hearts and motives were disconnected from God and His glory. We are often guilty of the same thing, both as individuals and in churches. We get consumed with doing the right things without considering why we're doing them (or doing them for selfish reasons). As churches, we quickly become institutions that place programs above people or the desire for the sweet spirit of Christ. A growing church can quickly become distracted with the necessary business of things and miss, even annihilate, the whole point, jeopardizing its DNA along the way.

Priorities can easily shift to chasing growth at all costs for any church. It is our nature to get consumed by ambitious leadership and bottom lines. Church can become a machine, where secular business tactics become necessary to maintain momentum, much less thrive. These all increase our risk of being pulled away from the countercultural manner of Christ.

And this is clearly not a numerical issue, as there are congregations of 50 that are completely off mission and churches of thousands that are totally on. This is not a style issue, a methodology difference, or a size distinction. It's a heart matter, the true barometer of genuine faith since the beginning of history.

Aware of this, King David constantly invited God to search his heart and the hidden motives within as he led the nation of Israel. The only thing worse than ignorance is being ignorant of our own ignorance, when we don't even know what we don't know. What we do know is that "the heart is deceitful" and can even fool its owner. Much damage can be inflicted from that place. We are easily distracted, losing perspective and reacting desperately, but no circumstance gives us license to discard the essentials: love, mercy, compassion, justice. The means do not justify the end when it comes to God's kingdom. *The means are everything*, the end is secondary. We don't obtain godly results through selfishness, greed, corruption, or ruthlessness; not through lying, misrepresenting, dividing, or slandering; nor through neglect, apathy, ego, or pride. If these patterns drive the manner in which we get from here to there, I don't care what it looks like when the dust settles; it's garbage.

Do you think it's easier to live with the end in mind or the means in mind? Why?

What about for a church? Why?

In general, if you were evaluated by the integrity of your means, not the end you finally achieved, what would people say?

God is unimpressed by the spiritual veneer or business savvy of faith communities and individual Christ-followers. We don't get to treat people like expendable articles and expect God to look the other way because it somehow advanced His kingdom or had nothing to do with it. We can't ignore God's ways and expect to maintain His favor. We don't get to neglect the major values of the gospel and claim preference or context. The demands of church leadership, but more importantly, of *living life* never come with a permission slip to act contrary to our heritage in Christ.

Read Isaiah 58:3-4. What pitfall plagued Israel?

How do you see that played out in your own life?

According to this passage, how does this struggle affect our communion with God?

In Isaiah 58:1, the Lord told Isaiah to raise his voice like a trumpet. Literally, God wanted Isaiah's voice to be like a *shofar*, a ram's horn used in religious celebrations and other special occasions in ancient Israel. For example, the shofar blowing would be a warning sign of advancing armies. Because God compared Isaiah's upcoming words to this rarely used and distinctive sounding instrument, He clearly wanted Isaiah's message to be immediate and to the point.

A whopping 90 percent of today's young adults believe they can have a good relationship with God without being involved in church. But 89 percent of young non-church-going adults said they would be willing to listen if someone wanted to tell them about Christianity. Numbers like these reveal that people are open to the gospel, but the church is failing to connect with the culture.

That Scripture sums up God's opinion rather completely. Not only was God the discarded lover in this scenario, wounded and heartbroken, but He'd attached His name to these people. They were the people chosen to represent the one true God for all the world to see. Not only did they reject Him, they defiled His reputation and delayed His fame. His kingdom was stunted, because His people were unavailable to fulfill His objectives. Though God desired the redemption of all nations, *no* nation had reason to be attracted to the God of Israel, since all they saw was the constant hypocrisy of Yahweh's people.

Does our duplicitous representation of Jesus not only assault Him but offend the rest of the world still? Is this partly why the church is declining in America? How could it not be? When we strike others on the same day we fast, we bring no integrity to the gospel. Unbelievers may not understand the nuances of our theology, but they know paying empty lip service to God is repulsive. We shouldn't expect our voices to be heard on high, and we had better get used to being ignored by people, too.

"People in America are not ignorant of Christianity," wrote Halter and Smay in *The Tangible Kingdom*. "They've heard the message, seen our churches on every corner, they flick by our Christian TV shows, they see our fish symbols on the backs of our cars. They've seen so much of pop Christian culture that they have a programmed response to us: *ignore, ignore, ignore*. What's needed is a change of parameters—something that will alter their emotional response."[42]

What is the most recent thing you've seen or heard a believer or a church say or do that got your attention in a good way?

What about it was refreshing to you?

Because our culture has put up a filter against Christian culture, we must realize that the "come and see" approach is no longer valid. In truth, we may have heart-felt, loving, compassionate programs in our churches, but we're going to be fighting years of baggage to get people there. How can we convince people to give the church one last chance?

A MODERN MESS

To attract our communities to Christ, we have to become missionaries, immersing ourselves in culture like yeast that might ultimately affect the whole batch. We are a sent people—missionaries in our neighborhoods, our kids' schools, our work places, our communities, our gyms, and our favorite restaurants.

The church is no longer central to a community, and therefore people are not drawn to it like they used to be. In our church planting effort, we couldn't expect anyone to heed us just because we hung out a church sign and donned the pastor label. We accepted that the first reaction we should anticipate was skepticism, and the only bridge through that chasm was through *sustained, genuine relationships*. Care of our fellow man, locally and globally, was our second best hope to attract people to our Jesus, far more effective than cool music or impersonal mailouts.

As missionaries have always understood, the key was to study the culture we were passionate to reach and submerge into that space with respect and love. Our mission field was south Austin, and no church planting method could be exactly transplanted into our context. We had to do the hard work of cultural immersion, so we put a for sale sign in our yard to move to the south side.

But getting into the culture is more than just changing geography. It's about shifting mindsets. Many of us, especially in the church world, are still operating from a modern mindset in a postmodern culture. Much ink has been spilled over this transition, but to sum up a few points, the modern mindset was launched during the Enlightenment in the 1700s, when "the lights went on."

People were governed by reason, intelligence, and scientific orientation. Knowledge was king, and they believed through scientific discovery and human reasoning, they could know everything or figure it out. This period was marked by extreme confidence in human ability, respect of authority, clear rights and wrongs, and individual rights.

Listen to "Resurrect Me" by Jon Foreman from the *Interrupted* playlist. Your group leader can e-mail you the whole playlist, or you can download it for free on the *Interrupted* product page of *LifeWay.com*, under "Support Materials."

Two of the most influential modernist thinkers were Charles Darwin, who put forth his theory of biological evolution, and Karl Marx, who argued that contrary to popular belief, workers in the capitalist system were anything but free.

Gene Edward Veith is the provost and professor of literature at Patrick Henry College, the director of the Cranach Institute at Concordia Theological Seminary, and the author of 18 books on different facets of Christianity and culture. Check out his blog at *geneveith.com* for frequent commentary and updates on postmodern culture.

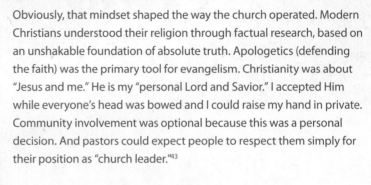

Obviously, that mindset shaped the way the church operated. Modern Christians understood their religion through factual research, based on an unshakable foundation of absolute truth. Apologetics (defending the faith) was the primary tool for evangelism. Christianity was about "Jesus and me." He is my "personal Lord and Savior." I accepted Him while everyone's head was bowed and I could raise my hand in private. Community involvement was optional because this was a personal decision. And pastors could expect people to respect them simply for their position as "church leader."[43]

Does that feel familiar to you? If so, which parts do you most closely identify with? If not, which parts are most unsettling?

From a modern standpoint, people came to church because they respected the institution and the pastor, they shared a clear interpretation of right and wrong that was not up for discussion, it was a safe place where they could belong, and they could navigate their faith without interference from others. Most churches upheld a modern worldview; indeed, because of their resistance to cultural influence, many still function with modern values in a society that no longer agrees with the tenets of that paradigm.

And therein lies the crucial shift.

AFTER THE MODERN

In the last 50 years, Western culture has undergone a transition to postmodernity, which challenges everything the modern paradigm holds dear. The 1960s amped up a process that was already underway. Following the assassinations of Martin Luther King Jr., John F. Kennedy, and Robert F. Kennedy, many Americans began fearing that even our finest leaders were vulnerable despite their knowledge and that the great progress of human rights might be reversed. Add the political chaos of the Vietnam War and the awareness that nuclear scientific advances could destroy us all, and people questioned their faith in science in light of the catastrophic destruction it made possible.

The postmodern worldview questions whether facts are completely knowable and whether logic is really the best tool with which to navigate life. Truth is no longer objective, concrete, observable; it is subjective and dependant on circumstances. For many postmoderns, the prominence of the individual is diminished. They think the personal pursuit of happiness should no longer be supreme; rather, the betterment of the community is a dominant value. Other variances of postmodernity include the following:

* Rationalism doesn't make a better society.
* Deconstruction reigns; there is no absolute truth that undergirds all of life.
* Everyone's story is a part of a bigger narrative.
* Postmoderns ask questions and challenge the status quo.
* Postmoderns have a global outlook in terms of responsibility for the ecology of the earth and its inhabitants.
* Since most postmoderns do not believe in absolute truth, judging is preposterous.
* Postmoderns are marked by a deep skepticism, and the twin ideas of power and control are repulsive.
* Answers to life's questions are never simple or simply reduced. Postmoderns believe life is messy, not easily dissected or understood.

How is this worldview hitting you? Which parts feel right to you?

Do any feel uncomfortable or incomplete?

There are obvious challenges for Christianity in the postmodern culture, but there's also a great deal of hope, particularly if we start to operate inside that culture rather than just running down its onset. In fact, if we start engaging postmodern conversations, there are a number of interesting values we find usable:

In his book *The New Tolerance*, Josh McDowell defines post-modernism as, "A worldview characterized by the belief that truth doesn't exist in any objective sense but is created rather than discovered. . . . [Truth] is created by the specific culture and exists only in that culture. Therefore, any system or statement that tries to communicate truth is a power play, an effort to dominate other cultures."[44]

* Scripture is applied in context of the needs of the community.
* Relationships are of utmost importance.
* Postmoderns tend to seek God in community rather than alone.
* Discipleship occurs over years in community.
* Authenticity is everything; the appearance of being slick, packaged, or over-produced is suspect.
* Postmoderns have been burned by positional authorities (government, parents, church leaders), so they are suspicious of establishment and must be won over by integrity, not title.
* Evangelism no longer emphasizes the rational, linear decision an individual makes at a specific point. It is a process, a journey, and a story.
* Postmoderns guard against consumerism and its effect on the church.
* How genuinely a church engages relief work and the care of global society is everything to a postmodern.[45]

Modernism said, "I have all the answers and so can you." Postmodernism responded, "I don't have all the answers and neither do you." So if culture is saying "apple" and the church insists on "orange," then big surprise: We're losing ground in society because we're not speaking the same language. "Evangelicals tend to disdain the culture and the language, preferring the old culture and language," wrote Mary DeMuth. "But it's not either/or; it's both/and. We aren't throwing the baby out with the bathwater; we're keeping the baby and changing the bathwater. The gospel remains the same, but the presentation changes."[46]

MISSION POSSIBLE

If we really want to connect inside our culture, then there are a few values we need to be unquestioningly dedicated to. Things like:

- A sense of global community and care for suffering humanity.
- Respect for our earth and its resources.
- Authenticity valued over appearance.
- A passion for community and honest relationships.
- Responsibility and the rejection of consumerism.

Not only are these the values of the average postmodern, but they completely align with the gospel. The best way to connect the gospel with our culture is to capitalize on the shared common ground. What if we really loved our neighbors and offered a safe place for community in our homes, *showing* them church rather than just *inviting* them to one? What if we served alongside secular nonprofits rescuing

Mary DeMuth is an expert in the field of pioneer parenting, a term used for parents who are trying not to make the same mistakes their parents made. She is the author of many fiction and non-fiction books, including *Authentic Parenting in a Postmodern Culture*. Her expertise stems largely from her childhood experiences, which are recounted on her Web site, *marydemuth.com*.

orphans? How might the church be perceived if we volunteered with organizations feeding the hungry? What if believers supported environmental groups working toward alternative fuel options? Could the very service Jesus required double as evangelism?

What are some other ways the postmodern mindset connects to the gospel?

Jump back to Isaiah and read 58:6. To advocate for justice, freedom, and restoration for the oppressed, what would you have to fast from?

This passage sounds like the postmodern rejection of individualism for community. Responsibility for each other is the first description of the fast God requires; an abstinence from selfishness, greed, and egotism. Discipleship is not a personal journey with few links to community; it exists to spur one another on toward liberation and execute justice for those too trapped to free themselves. It is a lifestyle obsessed with the broken members of our human tribe—those living next to us, in our families, and everywhere someone is devalued. We have a mandate to liberate our fellow man, in every context. We are in this life together; we belong to one another.

This is not just about doing church; it's about being the Church. I'm not talking about an infrastructure or strategy. I'm thinking of our core member who brings cakes to her neighbors every week. I'm thinking about eight of our families who took in total strangers evacuated from Houston thanks to Hurricane Ike; for a week, our people housed more than 80 evacuees who couldn't afford shelter, while the rest of our church brought food and supplies. I'm thinking about two of the men in our church who stood up in court with an abused single mom we met on the streets. And I'm thinking of the church member who volunteered to organize our downtown grill outs—his business savvy turned that mission into a well-oiled machine of efficiency.

For the definition of biblical community, look no further than Acts 2. In Acts 2:41, we find that Bible teaching, authentic relationships, fellowship, prayer, a strong bond of love and care for each other, and praise for God's goodness were common elements of this community. The threads of Christ's love bound them together as one.

At your small group meeting this week, watch the next installment of the documentary feature called "Interrupted—Part IV." The video segments are available for purchase on the *Interrupted* product page of *LifeWay.com*.

This is not about Brandon and Jen Hatmaker, church planters. This is about the bride of Christ; church simply provides the context for us to live on mission together. It's not about your church and how it is thrilling or failing you. Rather, what kind of bride are *you* helping to prepare? With the glorious addition of you and your gifts, is she becoming radiant? "There is a movement bubbling up that goes beyond cynicism and celebrates a new way of living," wrote Claiborne, "a generation that stops complaining about the church it sees and becomes the church it dreams of."[47]

Are you more prone to complaining or action? Why?

What is one action in your church context you sense God moving you to take?

SHARE, PROVIDE, CLOTHE, SHINE

Read Isaiah 58:7-10. Think of the deepest skeptic in your life. Would he or she be compelled by social justice?

How could you engage that person spiritually through compassion work?

How could this type of commitment cause our light to shine forth?

Not only is this the Jesus-language of Matthew 25, but it attracts the postmodern not moved by our buildings and events but by our social compassion and global impact. Mercy to the hungry, poor, homeless, and orphaned has the threefold advantage of administering relief to the most distressed, identifying with Jesus on the deepest level, and drawing the skeptic through an action he is already compelled by.

We've had people join us for social projects who would never join us for a church service. Our deepest cynic served burgers downtown with us six times before she set foot in church; she's a transformed believer now. Nonprofit leaders of secular organizations joined our community after our sustained service to their mission. We provide long-term care for a terminal couple with AIDS through The Care Communities; after five months they accepted Christ. The first person we baptized was a homeless woman we helped off the streets. One of our pastors was invited to speak about our mission initiative to all the employees at Wal-Mart after we forged a partnership for our Communities in Schools projects.

Our community work is not unprecedented. But it bears a meaningful witness to skeptics, nonbelievers, and the anti-organized religion population. What mailings, cold invites, media, and strategic marketing are struggling to still do, relationships through justice are accomplishing. It may disappoint the average consumer Christian, but it might be our only hope to convince the lost.

This is more vital than ever because although the postmodern values community and service, that doesn't mean he lives those values out. There is a marked difference between criticizing consumerism and actually resisting consumerism. It's en vogue to broadcast anti-materialism while Twittering via an iPhone, upgraded from last year's model. Crying "ecology" is one thing; making environment-friendly choices with money is another—the average carbon footprint remains high.

The marketing world panders to the postmodern rhetoric while selling to postmoderns under the table, capitalizing on their duplicity. The worldview postmoderns are drawn to is challenging to truly live by, not unlike the narrow path we are called to as Christ-followers— easy to talk about, hard to actually follow. The church must not only demonstrate its commitment to gospel-based values the postmodern shares, but show her how. Grab her by the hand and work alongside her.

The Care Communities (*interfaithcarealliance.org*) is a nonprofit organization in the Austin area that provides practical and compassionate support to people living with AIDS and cancer. Its vision is that no one will face a serious illness alone. Communities in Schools (*cisnet.org*) is a national organization dedicated to helping kids stay in school and prepare for life.

Read Isaiah 58:8-10. This is an if/then scenario. Which blessing on the obedient side of justice do you most hunger for? Healing? An end to a dark night of the soul?

Listen to "Captivate Us" by Christy Nockels from the *Interrupted* playlist. Your group leader can e-mail you the whole playlist, or you can download it for free on the *Interrupted* product page of *LifeWay.com*, under "Support Materials."

Do you see a link between your pain or confusion and the "ifs" in this passage?

Clearly, this is our business model. Why waste time on silly finger pointing when we have such worthy tasks to engage? I was going the way of Isaiah 58, Matthew 25, Luke 22, John 21. These made up the permanent address of light, healing, protection, communion, righteousness, answered prayers. Something fused together, and I was officially off the platform, launched into the adventure.

Our lives are too essential to waste on pettiness or word wars, greed or ladder climbing, anger or bitterness, fear or anxiety, regret or disappointment. Life is too short. We must run, not walk, the way of Isaiah 58, embracing authentic faith manifested through mercy and community. Living on mission requires nothing less. It is a grand adventure, a true voyage into the kingdom of God. Imagine if we all chose it.

Then our light would rise in the darkness indeed.

BRANDON'S TAKE

For the first time in our lives, we were simply trying to respond to the Spirit's leading. As I look back, I am convinced God was profoundly and specifically placing our hearts on kingdom work. On our journey, God shaped a clear foundation, and kingdom work, partnership, and focus were central. Although Jesus discussed the kingdom as much as any topic, it's something many believers have no concept of or affection for. Our focus naturally goes to our kingdom, our immediate reality, our goals and passions, and our church.

But that's not what Jesus taught. He told Peter in Matthew 16:18-19:

 "And I also say to you that you are Peter, and on this rock I will build My church, and the forces of Hades will not overpower it. I will give you the keys of the kingdom of heaven, and whatever you bind on earth is already bound in heaven, and whatever you loose on earth is already loosed in heaven."

Jesus never gave us the keys to His church—He handed over keys to the kingdom. This was Jesus' instruction: Place your affections on My kingdom and I will build My church. Bind your heart to things of eternal value, keep your mind on a vision bigger than you, and ensure all your efforts match those affections. Jesus will take care of the rest.

So we began to look for kingdom opportunities. God's plan started to unfold when we got a call from a complete stranger from a mission-minded denomination and culminated in a partnership that spanned across denominations, a city, and a nation just a few days later. We didn't know entirely what was going on (and are discovering new layers still). We just knew our thinking shifted, as did our way of doing church.

NOTES

INTERRUPTING YOUR LIFE

Here are some of the major influences in this part of Jen's story. To go further
with some of the ideas from this session, pick one out to dig into yourself:

* *The Tangible Kingdom: Creating Incarnational Community* by Hugh Halter and Matt Smay
* *unChristian* by David Kinnaman and Gabe Lyons
* *I'm Fine with God . . . It's Christians I Can't Stand* by Bruce Bickel and Stan Jantz
* *Leadership and Self-Deception* by The Arbinger Institute
* *Authentic Parenting in a Postmodern Culture* by Mary E. DeMuth
* Mobile Loaves & Fishes (*mlfnow.org*)

SESSION FIVE
SENT

I recently joined my kids for lunch at their school. My fourth grader, Gavin, had first lunch, so I sat with him and his fellow preteens for 20 minutes, enjoying deep discussions about gaming systems and online cheats (it's not as illicit as it sounds). A bonus was watching the girls attempt to get the boys' attention, while the guys stuck spaghetti noodles on their lips like mustaches, oblivious. There were a lot of "Dude!" comments, and several "That's so gay," after which Gavin glanced at me, silently begging me not to lecture his friends for that.

Every boy had shaggy soccer hair, styled some awkward 10-year-old way. (Gavin swoops his bangs across his forehead with mousse and calls it his "swaive." We don't know where he got this.) They were miniature teenagers; fashion conscious if not quite girl conscious, sarcastic, and so electronically sophisticated that their conversation sounded like a foreign language.

At your small group meeting this week, watch the final installment of the documentary feature called "Interrupted—Part V." The video segments are available for purchase on the *Interrupted* product page of *LifeWay.com*.

OUT OF KINDERGARTEN

Then I watched Caleb's kindergarten class walk in. All the 5-year-olds had their index fingers over their mouths, making the universal "I shall not make excessive noise" sign. Some of the little boys were holding hands. They carried Thomas the Tank Engine and Barbie Fairytopia lunchboxes. Those who spotted a parent started waving like Forrest Gump jumping off the "Jenny" shrimp boat. They unselfconsciously wore Disney Velcro shoes and outfits that communicated: "I dressed myself." I don't care what anyone says; kindergartners are large babies. Attending the same school as fifth graders should probably be illegal. Compared to the preteens, they were so precious and innocent, I could have burst into tears, risking swift ridicule from Gavin and his homies.

The growing up process is equal parts wonderful and painful. The changes are harder than I thought—and better than I thought. As much as I treasure the endearment of my kids' early childhood, I'm enjoying their developing maturity in other ways. My kids might not carry Thomas lunchboxes or call me Mommy anymore, but sometimes they slip and call me Dude, and that has its own charm too.

We quickly grew from the kindergarten, idealistic, innocent phase of church planting to the preteen, grittier, more realistic one. It was no longer the flawless concept tinged with perfection, but the coarseness had a new charm too. It began by getting our dream out of our heads and onto the ground; reality is sometimes a harsh teacher. And what a grand beginning: a handful of families meeting in an apartment complex, kids running helter skelter, each of us wondering if anyone knew what they were doing.

What spiritual adventure is on your plate right now?

What stage are you in? Early idealism? Messier reality? Realization? What is the best thing about the stage you're in?

In the case of our fledgling body of believers, we met once a week to dream, pray, and rally. And also to take care of the practical stuff—hello, reality. One of the first questions we had to deal with was naming our church.

We had several options. There were the directional names: Southwest Community, Northeast Fellowship, Westside Family, South Austin blah blah. Then there were the hip names: Faith Bridge, BridgePoint, CrossPoint, Guts Church, Flood Church, Hot Rod Church for Sinners.

We discussed this ad nauseam, and it finally emerged. We combed through a year's worth of prayers and journals and correspondence and Bible studies, and we remembered a consistent message:

- "We may serve *in the new way of the Spirit*" (Romans 7:6).
- "I give you a *new commandment*: love one another. Just as I have loved you, you must also love one another" (John 13:34).
- "For both circumcision and uncircumcision mean nothing; what matters instead is *a new creation*" (Galatians 6:15).
- "Put new wine into *fresh wineskins*" (Matthew 9:17).

Thus, Austin New Church was born, giving honor to this new covenant, new way, new love, new life.

Why did you choose to attend your church? Did you choose it because it meets your needs, or are you there because you're on board with its mission in your city?

If you answered "my needs," how are you feeling about your church?

If you answered "its mission," how are you feeling about your church?

There are six different Greek words translated "new" in the New Testament. *Kainos* is the Greek word used in these passages. When referring to form, *kainos* means "recently made, fresh, recent, unused, unworn." In reference to substance, it means "of a new kind, unprecedented, novel, uncommon, unheard of." The adjective "new" describing the wine in Matthew 9:17 is *neos* in Greek, meaning "youthful or fresh"; this is different than the *kainos* wineskins.

SENT

Austin New Church had some very specific goals for its mission. We wanted to raise up people who were more dedicated to Jesus than to a church or a leader. We wanted people to take ownership in their own spiritual development rather than exclusively relying on the church. We wanted to raise awareness of human suffering and lead people toward tangible opportunities to alleviate it. And we wanted to create not only disciples, but missionaries.

The idea of creating missionaries took the longest to develop. While we were saying "missional," most people thought that meant "mission," and I think we transposed the two for awhile as well. *Mission* encompassed our work with the homeless community, disadvantaged schools, an orphanage in Mexico, and a reforestation project in Africa. When we engaged some aspect of human suffering or care for the earth, it fell under the mission banner.

But even though all our mission work is sustained and long term, we spend the majority of our lives in our homes, our neighborhoods, at work, and in school. We felt it was essential to incorporate the *spirit of mission* into our natural habitats, where the brunt of our influence exists. To live missionally is just that—recognizing that you don't go on mission; your life is missional.

Teachers need to treat their schools like mission fields. Business leaders need to understand the principles of cultural immersion to reach their colleagues. Students have to develop language that attracts their skeptical classmates to Christ. Recovering legalists have to replace some entrenched perceptions about culture in order to become missionaries in their own neighborhoods. Taking Jesus seriously goes well beyond a church service or mission project; He becomes the substance of our whole lives.

Is it easier for you to live missionally or go on mission? Why? How do those two ideas fit together?

"As Christians we have all been sent by God to go into our own city and communities as missionaries. We are to be culturally entrenched and personally involved. We must incarnate Christ's life in our culture in order to impact this culture that is pagan in every way."
–Scott Thomas, Acts 29 Network, *acts29network.org*

Missional at its core means "sent." It is the opposite of "come to us." The core of the Great Commission is "go." We are to make disciples, but the prerequisite instruction is one of motion. Going is the noble history of the Trinity. God sent Jesus to dwell among fallen humanity—not to visit, not to remain separated, but to immerse. He was the Supreme Missionary to mankind, submerged in culture, among the people He wanted to rescue. Upon Jesus' resurrection, God sent the Spirit from the heights of heaven to the heart of every believer, an indwelling.

Among, beside, within—this is the way of the Trinity. God has gone to people since the day He walked in the garden. People only came to Him *after* an encounter, *after* a revelation, *after* belief. He is the initiator, meeting humans on their turf in the middle of their chaos. God understood that we were too broken and confused to find Him in His divine dwelling places. Once we belong to Him, we know where to look for sweet communion, but until then, He comes to us.

The Father sent Jesus, Jesus sent the Spirit, and together they send us as ambassadors for the gospel, immersed in humanity and living in the harvest field. On a practical level, why would we expect an unbeliever to come to church cold? What does he know of the beauty of the Spirit? Why would he be attracted to an unknown Savior or a community? Certainly there are the dechurched and rechurched with a context for God who might be attracted through familiar venues. But why would a cynic join a weekend celebration of a God he doesn't know?

The message must be brought to him, in his context, where he is and how he is. This, in fact, is the mission of the church. Missiologist Ed Stetzer wrote, "The church is one of the few organizations in the world that does not exist for the benefit of its members. The church exists because God, in his infinite wisdom and infinite mercy, chose the church as his instrument to make known his manifold wisdom in the world."[48]

Does that description of the church resonate with you? Why or why not?

When believers sequester from culture, it's like recruiting a group of traveling salesmen and discovering all they do is stay together at the office. Sure, they enjoy each other's company and share strong feelings for the product, but they're doing nothing to increase the fan base or generate new business. They've missed the whole point of their role.

For a more in-depth look at your role as a part of the missional church and how you can be the hands and feet of the body of Christ sent to change the world, check out *Sent* by Ed Stetzer at *threadsmedia.com*.

I used to reside in Christian subculture. I read James Dobson to learn how to parent, Dave Ramsey to learn how to budget, sang Third Day for inspiration, went to Women of Faith conferences for encouragement, consulted Christian Coalition guides to see how to vote, and read Tim LaHaye for my fiction fix. This was the controlled bubble I lived in with a few hundred of my closest friends. "Some call this the 'herding effect,'" wrote Stetzer. "When you are running in the middle of a herd of buffalo, everything looks identical. What we see becomes our reality. We think that everyone around us knows where we are, and they can come to church if they want to be like us."[49]

It's not that Christian influence is bad, but followed exclusively it distorts our perception of real life and our role in it. We develop a blind eye to the customs, cultures, communities, and contexts where people live their lives with different preferences and worldviews right next door to us. The problem with Christian segregation is that God asked us to be on mission with Him, to go to some group of people somewhere, and to minister to them in a way that meets *their* needs by speaking *their* language.

OFFERING A TANGIBLE KINGDOM

Authors Halter and Smay appropriately talk about what church should and should not be: "Church must not be the goal of the gospel anymore. Church should not be the focus of our efforts or the banner we hold up to explain what we're about. Church should be what ends up happening as a natural response to people wanting to follow us, be with us, and be like us as we are following the way of Christ."[50]

It's a great concept, but not one easily executed. We've relied on the church and the church staff to represent Jesus for so long, taking on that job leaves something of a vacuum. If the church staff isn't responsible for transformative life change in everyone's lives, how else will it happen?

Sunday attendance used to be the bullseye, but when the final goal is getting people to attend church, some unhealthy expectations are attached. The pastor becomes central, and too much hinges on his personality, teaching, and life. From pressure without and within, pastors learn to exhibit ideal caricatures of their real selves and forfeit authenticity for image. This has a trickle-down effect on the congregations, and honest community struggles to emerge.

And don't get me started on how much pressure is then put on the sermon. It becomes everyone's best hope to convince the skeptics in

Hugh Halter and Matt Smay are the founders and co-leaders of Missio, "a ministry of conversation and apprenticeship that empowers leaders to effectively engage their culture with the transformational news of Christ." Learn more at *mcap.info.*

our midst, which sometimes happens but often doesn't. How many sermons have actually altered your life? One 30-minute message a week is rarely the catalyst for transformation. Paul understood what drew people to faith:

"Instead we were gentle among you, as a nursing mother nurtures her own children. We cared so much for you that we were pleased to share with you not only the gospel of God but also our own lives, because you had become dear to us" (1 Thessalonians 2:7-8).

Message-centered evangelism leaves too much work to the paid pros and omits a meaningful relational context. Here are Halter and Smay again:

"When we focus on the message only, what are we saying to people? Maybe that they really aren't dear to us? Is it possible that to share four great truths about God without giving the listeners a part of our lives might communicate the wrong thing? Paul knew that a message without an attractive tangible person embodying and delivering it would fall on deaf ears or be lost amid all the other faiths of that time. What makes the gospel good news isn't the concept, but the real-life person who has been changed by it."[51]

How do you see the role of the pastor to the church?

Do you think your church hinges on the pastor and his messages? Why or why not?

If he quit or failed morally tomorrow, would there be enough to hold you at your church?

Rather than pinning all our hopes on a man with a microphone, how much more tangible is the gospel when someone experiences it over weeks and months with a real believer who they can ask questions

The New Testament distinguishes between two types of missionaries—those like Paul and those like Timothy. Paul emphasized spreading the name of Jesus to the world, while Timothy focused on local evangelism after people first heard the gospel. In other words, Timothy picked up where Paul left off. Loving your neighbor is answering the call to be a Timothy-like missionary.

of and learn from by observation? When a Christian consistently treats someone with compassion or demonstrates integrity at work, the gospel wins a hearing. We can continue to invite unbelievers to church, but we must first invite them into our lives. Have them over, go to dinner, welcome them in. Create a safe place for them to belong without having an agenda—they needn't worry about following our Christian rules yet (or pretending to in front of us). We must become their advocates, belonging with them as dear friends so they might one day feel comfortable belonging with us. The patient, hard work of love is the way of Christ. It's not a strategy for rapid church growth, but it is the subversive path into the kingdom.

The spirit of mission means that we serve our neighbors long before they are brothers or sisters in Christ. Putting their needs first, we sacrifice to love them. We act on their behalf, not with condescension as the Christian who has all the answers, but as their true friend. We can skip judging them; that's not our job. It isn't our responsibility to defend our values and prioritize our message over our posture. "Jesus didn't, and we shouldn't. He doesn't need us to stick up for him; he needs us to represent him, to be like him, to look like him and to talk like him, to be with people that he would be with, and to take the side of the 'ignorant' instead of those in the 'know.'"[52]

Love has won infinitely more converts than theology. The first believers were drawn to Christ's mercy way before they understood His divinity. That brings us back to the overemphasis on Sunday as the front door: If love is the most effective way, and the Bible says it is, then how much genuine love can one pastor show an entire congregation? His bandwidth is not wide enough, and when he fails to connect with every person (which he will), the congregation becomes disgruntled because he can't fulfill what should have been their mission. Nor can a random group of strangers standing in a church lobby offer legitimate community to some sojourner who walks in the door.

Believer, your pastor or your church can never reach your coworker like you can. They do not have the sway over your neighbor that has been entrusted to you. No one better than you can love your wayward brother. One decent sermon cannot influence a disoriented person like your consistent presence in her life can. While organized religion provokes mostly skepticism for the average postmodern, a genuine relationship with a Christ-follower on mission can reframe the kingdom, making a fresh perception possible. Then they discover that church is not a place you go to; it's a people you belong with. The building on Sunday is simply the place they celebrate God together.

How do you feel about this giant responsibility as a kingdom-minded Christ-follower?

Why do you think so few of us see ourselves in this light?

RIGHT TO REMAIN SILENT

Paul addressed the missional lifestyle better than any explanation I've ever heard:

Read 1 Corinthians 9:19. How would you re-word Paul's statement?

"For although I am free from all people, I have made myself a slave to all, in order to win more people" (1 Corinthians 9:19).

What do you think it means to be free from all people?

What do you think it means to be a slave to all people?

In a literal sense, a free person serves no other man. That is the basic meaning of free—he is not owned; he doesn't have to defer to another; he has rights and privileges because of his position. In fact, within the first-century context, a free man likely had servants to meet *his* needs; certainly not the other way around.

This freedom is the elevated station we are awarded at salvation. As free people, we are granted a new set of rights:

- We have the right to be called children of God, with the privileges that entails (John 1:12).
- We have the full rights of sons of God: We have His Spirit within us and we are heirs to the kingdom (Galatians 4).
- We have the right to eat from the tree of life and enter heaven's gates (Revelation 22:14).
- Astonishingly, we have the right to sit with Jesus on His throne one day (Revelation 3:21).
- We are free from the stranglehold of guilt and sin (Romans 6:22).
- We are free from legalistic human commands and teachings (Colossians 2).

By our adoption into the family of God, we become royalty. We have every privilege and right a king grants his children. We are free from conventional boundaries and enjoy exemptions because of our rank. It is within our entitlement to apply our advantages and live like the heirs we are.

This is all courtesy of Jesus, who forfeited His rights so we could have them instead.

What are the natural dangers of privilege and position?

How have you seen those play out in day-to-day life?

How about in a spiritual sense? How have you seen privilege and position misused?

When we assume the posture of a slave to all, we adopt the voluntary humility of Christ, who surrendered His rights for the salvation of mankind first. The literal implication of "slave" means we behave *like a real slave*—labor like one, defer to those we serve, are diligent to please and not offend, and act as if we have no privileges at all—to win as many as possible.

Matthew Henry wrote, "A heart warmed with zeal for God, and breathing after the salvation of men, will not plead and insist upon rights and privileges in bar to this design. Those manifestly abuse their power in the gospel who employ it not to edification but destruction, and therefore breathe nothing of its spirit."[53]

As we engage a broken world, standing stubbornly on principle or privilege indicates an immature heart that would rather be right than seek the redemption of his neighbor. When we lead with doctrine before love, we brutalize the spirit of the doctrine we're prioritizing. Insisting that unbelievers or disoriented believers defer to our convictions is the quickest way to repel them from God. We're leading with the wrong foot, and we might never get a chance to correct that offense.

But what if your neighbor came to understand that you *wanted* to be his servant? How would my colleague soften to the gospel if I set my agenda aside and became her constant slave? How would our communities be transformed if our churches became servants to our cities? If at every turn, believers labored for others like they were our masters, we could not be ignored for long.

> **Think of your most contentious relationship or aggressive skeptic. What could you immediately defer in order to become a better slave to that person?**

Matthew Henry was an English minister at the turn of the 18th century. He is best known for *The Exposition of the Old and New Testaments*, a six-volume commentary on the entire Bible. Henry worked on the book for the last 10 years of his life, getting through the book of Acts. It was finished by some of his fellow ministers after his death.

The mindset of "slave to all" must be the driving force in our relationships, especially with those who don't know Christ yet. We must go to *their* neighborhoods, to *their* homes, to *their* communities. We can't expect anyone to come to us, our faith community, or our church without a reason.

CHANGELINGS

Read 1 Corinthians 9:20-22. What do you think it meant to Paul to become like the Jews, living under the law?

How does that relate to us as missionaries?

Before he became Paul the apostle and writer of almost one-fourth of the New Testament, he was Saul, one of the most feared persecutors of Christians in the years following Jesus' resurrection. Paul's confession of his persecution is summed up in his defense before King Agrippa in Acts 26:9-11.

If I'm honest, I'll admit this part of missional living is much harder for me than engaging the most hostile skeptic. My own church background was one of obedience motivated by fear, so I am overly sympathetic to disoriented sojourners and unfairly impatient with fundamentalist evangelicals. My tolerance for silly rules and fear-based legalism is low, and I struggle with a very unmissional response to believers still living under a rigid law. But my background is nothing compared to Paul's. He truly knew what it was like to live under the bondage of the law as the Pharisee of Pharisees.

How honorable, then, that he wasn't compelled to lecture on Christian freedom and its liberties but respected other believers' convictions and joined their rituals. It was more important for Paul to win them to Jesus' mercy than to demonstrate his superior understanding of Jesus' freedom. Their legal restraints were love restraints for Paul, and his message was unpolluted by offensiveness.

If we're going to win people, then let's win people. We do whatever it takes—within the boundaries of law and biblical morality—to attract people to the glorious mercy of Jesus. When love regulates our liberty, we create a context to share the gospel where it can actually be received. If people are offended by God Himself, by His authority, His Word, His Son, His history, there is little we can do about that. They will ultimately have to wrestle with Him. But if they are offended by our representation of God, then we'll answer for our arrogance. We can help that, and we should.

We all have personal prejudices against this group or that, those who have burned us. But our emotions can't govern our message. We cannot stand on principle at any point along the belief spectrum. Whether persuading a legalist to grace or an atheist to faith, it is our high calling to innocently conform to their worldview in any possible way to earn a hearing for the gospel. Jesus ate with sinners, created wine for partygoers, fished with fishermen, held the children of mothers, taught in the temple with teachers, worshiped in synagogues with the faithful. All things to all people, not bound by convention, public opinion, appearance, or legalism—not even His own rights.

What kind of person was Paul describing in verses 21-22?

How might his approach to engaging someone like this have been different than the approach in verse 20?

Maybe it's my tattoos talking, but this is my favorite missional mandate. Because the perception of Christians as self-righteous segregationists is so prevalent, it is such a pleasure to represent a new expression of faith. For me this is not hard, this is not work, this is not a sacrifice, this is not uncomfortable. A missional approach to a disoriented world has made discipleship fun again.

And you know what? It's a lot more real. Living missionally begins with living more authentically for most of us. When you start to live on mission, you stop living with religious pretense treating people like potential converts, and you start living real life with them.

It's pretty fun.

I get to have dinner at a neighbor's house and later hear about her marriage struggles. Brandon organizes Neighborhood Texas Hold 'Em Nights to show those men another face of the pastorate; consequently, he's the first person they call in crisis. The eight families in our community group throw Halloween bashes and Christmas extravaganzas and potluck dinners and pool parties in our little subdivision. Our young married group throws birthday parties once a month for children with a parent in prison; they don't even have their own kids yet. One group invited women from their neighborhood to form a Race for the Cure team and run the 5K together.

Or how about these folks: We have a Hispanic newlywed couple who were so driven to impact their culture for Christ, Austin New Church rented them a house on the east side (entirely Spanish speaking and low income). Intentionally planted there, they invite neighbors into their home for dinners and parties; they hang out with the students

"All the tax collectors and sinners were approaching to listen to Him [Jesus]. And the Pharisees and scribes were complaining, 'This man welcomes sinners and eats with them!'" (Luke 15:1-2).

Visit *southaustincares.org* for the growing list of Austin New Church's local and global partnerships.

who attend the elementary school across the street. They organize neighborhood cleanups and work with the school administration. They both have real jobs; this is just their life. They don't "do missions"; they are missionaries living in the harvest field they've been sent to. That's the key, isn't it? To stop "doing" and start "being"?

Do you see the difference in "doing" and "being"? What does that difference mean to you?

See Matthew 20:16, 20:27; Mark 9:35; and 2 Corinthians 5:17 for more verses that support these statements.

"I'M NOT BEING FED"

If the focus of our lives is on *going*; if we are really driven by becoming all things to all people . . . what about us? When do we "get fed"? What about our spiritual growth?

Do we really believe when God called us to live missionally, He didn't consider this? Maybe we have misunderstood what being fed is all about. We think of it as having our needs met, our intellects challenged, learning Scripture. Undoubtedly those things are part of being fed. The question is how those things happen. Is it possible that in God's design for spiritual maturity, being fed actually links up with becoming a slave to all people?

The largest factor in feeling unfed is not feeding others. It has less to do with your pastor's preaching style or the curriculum you're studying. You could serve your church campus ten hours a week and still feel undernourished, because we have an innate craving to live on mission with God in the dangerous, exciting world. It's out there where we get over ourselves; where we are fed. That seeming contradiction fits nicely with other biblical paradoxes:

You are first when you become last.
You are great when you become least.
You live when you die.

Is it really a stretch to realize you get fed when you are feeding others, giving yourself away fully and completely for the mission of God? Fulfillment exists in becoming a slave to everyone to win someone to Jesus.

How would you define "getting fed"?

How do you feel about redefining it in terms of giving yourself to the service of others? Why?

Do we really need another sermon? I've heard 10 million sermons in my life, yet almost none of my transformational moments took place in a church pew. For me and countless others, transformation occurred not in the form of a brilliant teacher showing me the latest original language treasure in the Word. Not in another Bible study that finally cured my spiritual glitches. Not from writing another book or reading someone else's. Not from one second spent on a church campus.

Transformation came in the form of dirty homeless men and abandoned orphans. It came through abused women and foster kids. It came through lost neighbors crying at my kitchen table. Transformation began with humility, even humiliation. It started with conviction and discipline. It increased through loss, not gain. It grew through global exposure and uncomfortable questions. It was born out of rejection, replanted in new soil. It was not found in my Christian subculture but in the eyes of my neighbors, the needs of my city, the cries of the nations. It was through subtraction, not addition, that transformation engulfed me, and I'll tell you something:

I am not the same.

Amazingly, missional living doesn't just benefit "those" people—it is the path to making true disciples of those participating in it. If an endless array of Bible studies, programs, church events, and sermons have still left you dry, please hear this: Living on mission *where you've been sent* will transform your faith journey. At the risk of oversimplifying it, I've seen missional living cure apathy better than any sermon, promote healing quicker than counseling, deepen discipleship more than Bible studies, and create converts more effectively than events.

It transforms both the master and the slave.

"I pray that you, being rooted and firmly established in love, may be able to comprehend with all the saints what is the length and width, height and depth of God's love, and to know the Messiah's love that surpasses knowledge, so you may be filled with all the fullness of God" (Ephesians 3:17-19).

Are you on mission and surrounded by others who are too? Where?

If yes, what transformation is God engineering in you right now? What is shifting?

If no, do you struggle with spiritual boredom, dissatisfaction, or a critical spirit? Is there a connection?

"Passion for God in worship precedes the offer of God in preaching. You can't commend what you don't cherish. Missionaries will never call out, 'Let the nations *be glad!*' who cannot say from their heart, '*I rejoice* in the LORD . . .' Missions begins and ends in worship."
–John Piper[54]

When it comes to effective church outreach, one size does not fit all. There are cultural codes that must be broken for all churches to grow and remain effective in their specific mission context. *Breaking the Missional Code* by Ed Stetzer provides expert insight on church culture and church vision casting, plus case studies of successful missional churches impacting their communities.

There is no formula to living on mission. What works in my middle-class neighborhood in South Austin might be the weirdest thing in the world for your affluent urban community. There is no such thing as: "Week One—invite neighbor to dinner. Week Two—organize a book club with work friends. Week Three—work with a nonprofit. Week Four—serve the poor. This is the winning schedule."

Those tactics might be wildly successful in one place and fall flat in another. Formulas tend to fixate on the details and accidentally miss the point, so don't transplant our vision into your context without breaking the code for your specific culture.

But there is no magic to living on mission, either. Speak the language of the people you're sent to; that's pretty much it. When you can, value what they value, enjoy what they enjoy, go where they might go, think like they might think. Connect with them on their terms, not yours. If you live around intellectuals, that's your avenue; the Bible should keep them occupied for the rest of their lives. If you live in a creative community, connect through the arts; they'll ultimately discover the beauty of God to be overwhelming. If music, then music. If sports, then sports. Be it books, movies, conversation, exercise, hunting, parenting, social work, community activism, camping, coffee, good food, or any good thing, decode the love language of the tribe around you and speak it. It's not rocket science. Win them over to you, and you'll have the best chance to win them over to Christ.

What is the love language of the tribe around you?

What are some easy ways to speak that language and connect with them to ultimately win a hearing for the gospel?

WHAT'S IN IT FOR ME?

But maybe you've still got that nagging question, "What's in it for me?" If you do, you're not alone. We ask that question because many of us still think the church is exclusively for us, and other people can enjoy its advantages when they choose to join it. Those benefits are things like assurance of heaven, growing in intimacy with Jesus, living with hope, and countless other goodies. But there are other benefits, too . . .

Read 1 Corinthians 9:22-23. What benefits to ourselves do you think we forego when we're off mission?

Paul declared his voluntary slavery to all; he gave himself away totally for the sake of the kingdom. And yet in doing so, he shared in the benefits of the gospel. It seems counterintuitive; you might imagine Paul's slavery meant forfeiting benefits, but he said the opposite. It is through preferring the bottom—choosing slavery—that he actually experienced the benefits of kingdom dwelling. I'm starting to understand what that means. I'm sharing in the blessings of the gospel more now than I have in my entire life.

Activists Shane Claiborne and Jonathan Wilson-Hartgrove show how prayer and action must go together in *Becoming the Answer to our Prayers*. Their exposition of key Bible passages provides concrete examples of how a life of prayer fuels social engagement and the work of justice. If you hope to see God change society, you must be an ordinary radical who prays—and then is ready to become the answer to your own prayers.

It's fitting that "slave" is from a group of words meaning "bonded," which is the same root word used in Titus 2:3 about women addicted to wine. In other words, as slaves to our neighbor, our cities, the people of the nations, we are addicted to them. We cannot get enough of them in our homes, in our lives. The more we love them, the more we want to love them. We are addicts for mission, bonded to people for the dream of the gospel in their lives.

Now that's a benefit.

This is the mission we are all called to, believers—it's the noble task of the church. It's not enough to be theologically brilliant without the heart of a missionary. It's sometimes intangible work planted in the messy soil of relationships instead of the cleaner territory of theology. It's slow, often maddening. It requires the patience of Job and the maturity of Paul to execute the mission of Jesus. Living on mission will be misinterpreted and criticized—count on it.

Amid the fabric of community and developing relationships, you'll often wonder if this is doing anything for the kingdom. But you'll remember it is when your neighbor in crisis rings your doorbell at 1 a.m. You'll be more convinced when they are drawn to the beauty of Jesus after witnessing His kingdom consistently breaking through in your life. Weeks, months, years—we are bonded to people as long as it takes. The battle is for the souls of humanity, and our secret weapon is love. The King and His kingdom will reign supreme—that is settled. The only question is: Will you help contend for it?

Dr. King said it best at the Prayer Pilgrimage for Freedom in 1957: "When the history books are written in the future, the historians will have to look back and say, 'There lived a great people . . . a people who injected *new meaning* into the veins of civilization . . . a people that gave *new integrity* and *a new dimension of love* to our civilization.' When that happens, the morning stars will sing together, and the sons of God will shout for joy."[55]

It's the "new" the whole world is waiting for.

The Prayer Pilgrimage for Freedom took place on May 17, 1957. More than 30,000 people from more than 30 states gathered at the Lincoln Memorial in Washington, D.C., to celebrate the three-year anniversary of the desegregation of schools and to pressure states to implement the court-ordered ruling. It was at this event that Martin Luther King Jr., gave his first speech before a national audience. At the time it occurred, the march was the largest Civil Rights demonstration.

BRANDON'S TAKE

God changed the trajectory of our lives. I was feeling something my spirit had been craving, something that was missing. My entire Christian journey, I've felt one click away from full, one click away from true joy, one click away from contentment. Reluctant to admit it, I had a constant desire for more, a nagging hope to be "fed" beyond what I was experiencing.

Paul prayed for the Ephesians:

"I pray that you, being rooted and firmly established in love, may be able to comprehend with all the saints what is the length and width, height and depth of God's love, and to know the Messiah's love that surpasses knowledge, so you may be filled with all the fullness of God" (Ephesians 3:17-19).

If we've been in church for years yet aren't full, are we really hungry for more knowledge? Do we really need another program or event? Do we need to be fed more of the Word, or are we simply undernourished from an absence of living the Word? If our faith is about us, then we are not just hungry—our spirits are starving.

In Ephesians 4, Paul wrote that if we prepare ourselves for works of service, we will become mature, complete, perfected, and not lacking in anything. Isn't that what we're looking for?

In John 13, Jesus washed the disciples' feet and closed this physical parable with these words:

"I have given you an example that you also should do just as I have done for you. I assure you: A slave is not greater than his master, and a messenger is not greater than the one who sent him. If you know these things, you are blessed if you do them" (John 13:16-17).

NOTES

INTERRUPTING YOUR LIFE

Here are some of the major influences in this part of Jen's story. To go further with some of the ideas from this session, pick one out to dig into yourself:

* *Planting Missional Churches* by Ed Stetzer
* *Breaking the Missional Code* by Ed Stetzer and David Putman
* *Organic Church* by Neil Cole
* *A Call to Conscience: The Landmark Speeches of Dr. Martin Luther King, Jr.*

NOTES

END NOTES

SESSION 1

1. Shane Claiborne, *The Irresistible Revolution* (Grand Rapids, MI: Zondervan, 2006), 39.
2. Clayborne Carson and Kris Shepard, eds., *A Call to Conscience: The Landmark Speeches of Dr. Martin Luther King, Jr.* (New York: Warner Books, 2001), 213-214.
3. Jeffrey Sachs, *The End of Poverty* (New York: Penguin Books, 2005), 18.
4. Ibid., *The End of Poverty*, 18.
5. Anup Shah, "Poverty Facts and Stats," September 3, 2008, *http://www.globalissues.org/article/26/poverty-facts-and-stats*.
6. *http://www.callandresponse.com/about.html*
7. *http://www.worldorphans.org/problem/index.htm*
8. George H. W. Bush, quoted in Jack Beatty, "Playing Politics with the Planet," *Atlantic Unbound* (April 14, 1999), *http://www.theatlantic.com/unbound/polipro/pp9904.htm*.
9. "Weblog: Joel Osteen vs. Rick Warren on Prosperity Gospel," compiled by Ted Olson, *Christianity Today*, posted September 14, 2006, *http://www.christianitytoday.com/ct/2006/septemberweb-only/137-41.0.html*.
10. *http://www.time.com/time/magazine/article/0,9171,1533448,00.html*
11. *http://www.letusreason.org/Wf45.htm*
12. *http://www.time.com/time/magazine/article/0,9171,1533448,00.html*
13. *http://www.brainyquote.com/quotes/quotes/m/q107529.html*
14. "Powell sees eradicating poverty as real fight against terrorism," *Kyodo News International*, December 29, 2004, *http://findarticles.com/p/articles/mi_m0XPQ/is_2004_Dec_29/ai_n8588523*.
15. *http://foundationcenter.org/getstarted/faqs/html/givingstats.html*
16. *http://www.adherents.com/Religions_By_Adherents.html*
17. Robert F. Kennedy, address of the Day of Affirmation: "It is from the Numberless," University of Capetown, South Africa, June 6, 1966.
18. Donna Bordelon Alder, "How to Encourage Your Pastor's Wife," *http://www.parsonage.org/articles/married/A000000065.cfm*.

SESSION 2

19. Max Anders, *Holman New Testament Commentary, Luke*, vol. 3 (Nashville: Broadman and Holman Publishers, 2000), 80.
20. *http://dictionary.reference.com*
21. Chad Brand, Charles Draper, and Archie England, eds., *Holman Illustrated Bible Dictionary* (Nashville: Holman Bible Publishers, 2003), 335.
22. Walter J. Harrelson, ed., *New Interpreter's Study Bible* (Nashville: Abingdon Press, 2003), 1896.
23. Ibid., *Holman Illustrated Bible Dictionary*, 1052.
24. Ibid., *Holman Illustrated Bible Dictionary*, 185.
25. Ibid., *The Irresistible Revolution*, 127.
26. Richard Rohr, *Simplicity* (New York: NY: The Crossroad Publishing Company, 1991), 144.
27. Ibid., *Holman Illustrated Bible Dictionary*, 968-69.

SESSION 3

28. The Barna Group, Ltd. "Twentysomethings Struggle to Find Their Place in Christian Churches." *http://www.barna.org*. September 24, 2003.
29. The Barna Group, Ltd. "Spirituality May Be Hot in America, but 76 Million Adults Never Attend Church." *http://www.barna.org*. March 20, 2006.
30. Tom Clegg and Warren Bird. *Lost in America* (Loveland, CO: Group Publishing, 2001), 27.
31. *http://www.barna.org/FlexPage.aspx?Page=Resource&resourceID=53*
32. Ibid., *Lost in America*, 29.
33. *http://www.churchcentral.com/article.php?id=774*
34. *http://www.churchcentral.com/article.php?id=536*
35. Ibid., *Lost in America*, 57-58.
36. Hugh Halter and Matt Smay, *The Tangible Kingdom* (San Francisco, CA: Jossey-Bass, 2008), 9-10.
37. *www.cs.rice.edu/~ssiyer/minstrels/poems/1595.html*
38. Ibid., *Simplicity*, 57.

SESSION 4

39. *http://www.freemethodistchurch.org/sections/resources/free/classics/EC_1.shtml*
40. Thomas L. Constable, "Notes on Isaiah," (2008 Edition), 260; *http://soniclight.com/constable/notes/pdf/isaiah.pdf*.
41. Oswalt, John N. *The Book of Isaiah, Chapters 40–66*. (Grand Rapids: Wm. B. Eerdmans Publishing Co., 1998) 497.
42. Ibid., *The Tangible Kingdom*, 125.
43. Ibid., *The Tangible Kingdom*, 61-75; Mary E. DeMuth, Authentic Parenting in a Postmodern Culture (Eugene, OR: Harvest House Publishers, 2007), 22-23.
44. Josh McDowell and Bob Hostetler, *The New Tolerance: How a Cultural Movement Threatens to Destroy You* (Carol Stream, IL: Tyndale House Inc., 1998) 208.
45. Ibid., *Authentic Parenting in a Postmodern Culture*, 24-27.
46. Ibid., *Authentic Parenting in a Postmodern Culture*, 27.
47. Ibid., *The Irresistible Revolution*, 24.

SESSION 5

48. Ed Stetzer, *Breaking the Missional Code* (Nashville, TN: Broadman and Holman Publishers, 2006), 44.
49. Ibid., *Breaking the Missional Code*, 33.
50. Ibid., *The Tangible Kingdom*, 30.
51. Ibid., *The Tangible Kingdom*, 42.
52. Ibid., *The Tangible Kingdom*, 46.
53. Matthew Henry, *Matthew Henry's Commentary on the Whole Bible: Acts to Revelation*, vol. 6, *http://www.ccel.org/ccel/henry/mhc6.iCor.x.html*.
54. John Piper, *Let the Nations Be Glad!: The Supremacy of God in Missions* (Grand Rapids: Baker Academic, 2003), 17.
55. Ibid., *A Call to Conscience*, 56.

LET'S BE FRIENDS!

VISIT OUR LIFEWAY WOMEN'S BLOG AT
lifeway.com/allaccess